News Writing

News Writing

Anna McKane

S SAGE Publications
London ● Thousand Oaks ● New Delhi

First published 2006

SAGE Publications Ltd
1 Oliver's Yard
55 City Road
London EC1Y 1SP

SAGE Publications Inc.
2455 Teller Road
Thousand Oaks, California 91320

SAGE Publications India Pvt Ltd
B-42, Panchsheel Enclave
Post Box 4109
New Delhi 110 017

British Library Cataloguing in Publication data

A catalogue record for this book is available
from the British Library

ISBN-10 1-4129-1914-2   ISBN-13 978-1-4129-1914-2
ISBN-10 1-4129-1915-0 (pbk)   ISBN-13 978-1-4129-1915-9

Library of Congress Control Number: 2006924529

Typeset by C&M Digitals (P) Ltd, Chennai, India
Printed in Great Britain by The Cromwell Press Ltd, Trowbridge, Wiltshire
Printed on paper from sustainable resources

CONTENTS

FOREWORD

The final stage of the journalistic process, the only one the audience encounters directly, is the words. They may be printed, spoken, or placed on a computer screen, but first they have to be prepared, and that usually means written. If they are boring, they will bore. If they are incomprehensible, they will not be understood. If they are clumsy, or illiterate, or ungrammatical, or inappropriate, they will annoy. No matter how good the reporting, how dramatic the revelation, how brave, despicable, corrupt, extraordinary or inspirational the events described, if the writing does not engage the audience all that came before it is wasted.

Keith Waterhouse, in his *Waterhouse on Newspaper Style* (Viking, 1989, now sadly out of print), still one of the best books on newspaper writing there is, lamented the decline of written English as practised by the "new mass middle class". In his book, which started life in 1979 as an in-house style guide for *Daily Mirror* journalists, he reflects: "Middle class tastes, never very high, are lowering all the time under the influence of the mass media and consumer advertising and with the decline in educational standards. Good prose is not a first requirement; a good home computer page is."

Good prose, good news writing, can be taught. And needs to be. Most journalists today emerge from journalism courses where the reporting skills are taught. The most demanding of these is writing, and most of us in journalism education find there is a lot of time-consuming work to be done in this area. However bright the students, learning how to write for publication is challenging.

The easiest thing is to give them examples of bad writing: bureaucratese; police speak; letters from banks and local authorities; wriggling defences from the providers of goods and services. Some of the worst comes in internal communication with companies and organisations. Sadly one cannot exclude the academy. In an age when the word communication is a cliché, and we have allegedly never done more of it, the language is seldom fit for purpose. Jargon and obfuscation reign.

Journalism's role is to inform, and a by-product of that is that journalism's job is to look after the means of doing that, the language, the writing. Anna McKane makes her daily contribution to that in her teaching, her rigorous, repetitive insistence on high standards. I have seen it at close hand, the devices she employs, her patient explanation of what the student could do to make it better, her ability to disguise pedantry (not a pejorative, in my book, where news writing is concerned) through clever examples. This book shares all that with a wider audience.

Employers talk constantly of their need for clear, organised prose. These are not just media employers. Journalism students leave their courses, or should, with that most transferable of transferable skills, the ability to put it across concisely and accessibly. It equips them for a wide range of employment.

For journalists it is, simply, the most vital tool. It is why, for all their faults, newspapers serve the language, use the language effectively, more than most that is written. For them it is entirely pragmatic and commercial. It all comes down to readability. Does good writing sell? I don't know. But if the writing grabs the reader, makes them want to read on, makes them enjoy what they are reading, then that writing certainly sells. And is probably good writing.

Peter Cole
Professor of Journalism, University of Sheffield

PREFACE

This book derives from my 20 years as a full-time journalist, mainly for Reuters, and my 12 years teaching at City University, where I have developed a news writing course based on my professional work.

I believe that the ability to write an accurate and lively news story is the cornerstone of a successful career as a journalist. Of course plenty of people want to become feature writers, sub-editors, or commissioning editors. But even for them, I think the ability to spot the news angle in an event, and order the material to make a coherent news story, is fundamental, and those skills will be useful in every other area of journalism. Feature writers may well need some news writing techniques for some types of feature, and subs and other editors will need to be able to spot when someone else's story is a good or a bad one.

There are plenty of good books about interviewing, and plenty which cover the problems and pitfalls of reporting, but I have not found one which covers in a detailed step by step approach how to write a basic news story. If an inexperienced journalist follows through this book, she will end up with a publishable story.

Chapter 1 gives some guidance on how to recognise a news story, and how to work out whether it is right for your publication. We did a detailed analysis of the national newspapers over two days to back up the ideas I already had about the two elements which are in almost every news story: conflict and people.

Chapter 2 covers the pitfalls and problems associated with gathering the news. The actual craft of reporting, research and interviewing, are outside the scope of this book, and there are several others which cover these areas. Some are listed in Appendix 2. Chapter 3 explains how to write a basic hard news intro (meaning introduction, the first paragraph) with examples and explanations of why certain approaches work better than others. I have found that with an hour to write a short story of about 200 words, an inexperienced reporter needs to spend almost 20 minutes on the first sentence. If that is right, the rest of the story will fall into place.

Chapters 4, 5 and 6 all cover the structure of the story. The first sets out and illustrates the inverted pyramid, which is used in most journalism training to illustrate the way a news story is structured. Chapters 5 and 6 derive from my teaching: I have developed the 'news story as answers' idea, as another way to try to help students work out what piece of information to put into each paragraph.

Chapter 6, 'Avoiding Narrative', was also developed from my teaching, when I discovered that sometimes when writing a complicated story about a chain of events, the students end up with a narrative rather than a news story.

Chapter 7 covers other news writing models, and Chapter 8 discusses the all important need for accuracy.

Chapters 9 and 10 deal with language. Chapter 10 gives advice on tight writing. Avoiding unnecessary words is essential in journalism, and is of great value in every other kind of writing as well. At the same time news stories need to be colourful and arresting, and this is covered in Chapter 9, with examples from a variety of sources.

Chapter 11 covers the main points of grammar which trainee journalists would need to know. I have covered all the points which through my teaching I have discovered can cause problems, and have avoided the rules of grammar which some books still stick to, but which are rapidly disappearing in the real world.

Chapter 12 gives an essential view from the point of view of the sub-editors. Too few reporters take the trouble to understand the constraints on the production team, or to acknowledge the huge contribution made on the subs' table.

The final chapter explains some of the other material which appears on news pages, so that if you are asked to provide a fact box or a chronology, you will know what is required.

The appendix sets out all the news stories in the national newspapers on July 18 and 19, 2005. It was great fun working out which papers covered which stories and trying to work out why. Why did the *Daily Star* give only a couple of paragraphs to the death of Edward Heath? Did they believe the majority of their readers had forgotten who he was? Why did the *Guardian* cover a couple of not very interesting stories about the BBC? Was it because a lot of their readers are media folk? It was fascinating to see how papers angle stories. The story of the conviction in London of Afghan warlord Faryadi Zardad for crimes committed in Afghanistan was reported in some papers, such as *The Times*, in a fairly straight way which would automatically put it into the conflict category. The *Daily Mail* chose to emphasise the cost to the British taxpayer of keeping him in jail here, thus giving the story elements of the relevance to the reader category. Most papers carried short stories about Hurricane Emily, but whereas the *Independent*, for example, ran a fairly straight story about 85,000 people being evacuated from their homes in Mexico, the *Daily Star* homed in, with a picture, on British tourists at the airport in Cancun.

There are many legal pitfalls for journalists, but they are outside the scope of this book. Students should study the various books on media law.

Apologies to all the men reading this, but to save the clumsy phrase 'he or she' or the expression s/he I have referred throughout to reporters, news editors, interview subjects and everyone else as 'she'. I realise this is not ideal, but I think it is preferable to the UGASP (ungrammatical gender ambiguous singular pronoun: see Chapter 11) in such expressions as 'a journalist should always check their sources'.

ACKNOWLEDGEMENTS

Thanks to Christopher McKane for writing Chapter 12 giving the view from the subs' table, and for looking through and commenting on everything else. Thanks to Jamila Ahmed for helping with the original idea, and to Sandra Jones for editing the manuscript so carefully. Thanks to colleagues and former colleagues Paul Anderson, James Anslow, Adrianne Blue, Harriett Gilbert, Jonathan Hewett, Melanie McFadyean, Ann McFerran, Sarah Niblock, Barbara Rowlands, Barbara Schofield, and Rosie Waterhouse for advice, ideas and for helping me to cope with stress.

Thanks to Syma Tariq for her research on news stories, and to all present and former students for their ideas and enthusiasm.

Thanks to the following publications for permission to quote their stories:

- *Restaurant* magazine for 'F me it's Gordon' in Chapter 4
- The *Daily Mail* for 'Fury as minister takes a swipe at studying the arts' in Chapter 5
- The *Financial Times* for 'Taipei fury at China's "disprespectful" panda offer' in Chapter 9
- The *Guardian* for 'Eagle landed: Graf Spee emblem salvaged'.

1 WHAT MAKES NEWS?

Experienced journalists seem to have news sense flowing in their blood. It is hard for them to imagine *not* being able to spot what makes a good news story, and hard for them to imagine that a trainee can't spot it. Maybe all students and trainees have to face having their ideas rejected a few times, to help them work out what exactly makes news. One of the most-quoted definitions of news is that of William Randolph Hearst, the press baron who was the model for Orson Welles's Citizen Kane:

> News is something somebody wants suppressed – all the rest is advertising.

This sounds impressive but actually it is nonsense: no one wanted to suppress the stories of the sinking of the Titanic, the ascent of Everest, or the tsunami.

Charles Dana, an editor of the *Sun,* in New York, during the 19th century said:

> News is anything which interests a large part of the community and which has never been brought to their attention.

This stresses the two most obvious points: it needs to be something that would interest your readers, and if they already know it, then it is not news. The first of these two criteria pinpoints one of the reasons why it can be hard for beginners to work out what is news: they need to put themselves in their readers' shoes. They need to understand their readers and decide exactly what they are interested in. Whether you are working for a magazine aimed at the hotel trade, a small local paper or a national paper, it is essential that you picture your average reader and work out what news she will be interested in.

It is probably easiest to work out what kind of news is needed in magazines aimed at a particular industry. These used to be known as trade magazines, and now they are usually called **B2B** (business to business).

Developments within the industry, such as takeovers or mergers of big firms, news involving the well-known people in the industry, political developments which might affect the industry, these are all the kinds of stories that will interest the readers.

The news for local papers might be a bit harder to analyse. It comes down to events that happen in the area, and events that affect people within the area. Local papers tend to work to very strict borders: quite a large news event just outside the circulation area will not be covered at all, unless people from within the area are affected. Then the second thing to think about is the **threshold** or scale of the event. It is easy to see that a big dramatic event (families evacuated because of burst water main) will make a news story, and a very much smaller but quirkier event (pet snake escapes) will also make it into the paper. The in-between stories can be seen as being on a sliding scale: if a lot of potential readers are affected (school closing) it will get in, if few people are (café closing) it might not. Then again, if it was a well-known poetry café, or the owner was a well-known character, it would get in.

Local papers tend to have unwritten rules which it will take a while for an inexperienced reporter to learn: it may be that car crashes are reported only if someone is killed, for example, or house fires only if the damage is so bad that the family has to be evacuated. The news in national newspapers is the hardest to pin down, and there have been several attempts over the years to do so.

The most commonly cited list of news values was drawn up by two Swedish sociologists, Johan Galtung and Mari Ruge, in 1965. Some of them look blindingly obvious, but the list does still incorporate most stories that get into newspapers and magazines. And if a story does not fit at least some of the criteria on the list, it probably is not news. I have rearranged their list into three groups: (1) criteria that relate to the occurrence of the event (the when and where for example); (2) criteria that are about the nature of the event itself, that is what events are considered newsworthy; and (3) criteria which might be said to be about the treatment of the events.

CRITERIA RELATING TO THE OCCURRENCE OF AN EVENT

FREQUENCY

This is the term usually used, but perhaps *timescale* would be better. It means that for it to be newsworthy, the event must have happened very recently. It must have happened since the publication we are working for last went to press. So for a monthly magazine, it would be within the past month.

For a daily, it would generally be the day before. Evening papers are especially keen to have every story, especially in later editions, about something that happened that very day.

There is an exception to this, however, and that is when information becomes available now about something that happened a while ago. The best example of this is when Cabinet and other papers are released to the public decades after the events. So we get stories about decisions Churchill made during the 1940s suddenly popping up on the news pages.

THRESHOLD

This means the scale of the event. The bigger the earthquake, the more Cabinet members are sacked, the bigger the tax change, the bigger the story. This point is often nowadays described, for example by Sarah Niblock in *Print Journalism: A Critical Introduction* (Keeble (ed.), 2005), as *impact*. The scale of the event in relation to the publication's readership is also relevant: a late-night pub brawl in which someone was killed would be big news for the local paper, would possibly get on to local evening TV, but would not get into the national papers unless there were a strange quirk about it, or a well-known person was involved or was a witness: 'A Coronation Street star watched in horror as …'

CRITERIA RELATING TO THE NATURE OF AN EVENT

UNEXPECTEDNESS

The more unlikely an event is, the more it will be news. This again is pretty obvious, although on its own it doesn't tell us much. I hate bicycles, so it is highly unlikely that I would ride one, but even if I did, it wouldn't be news. To be news, an unexpected event has to fit some of the other criteria as well. It is also highly unlikely that I would do a parachute jump, but if I did, that probably would make news for the local paper: the event itself is unexpected, but it is also rare.

ELITE PERSONS

We would now call them celebrities. This is the one point which is driving the news agenda now much more than it did 40 years ago. *The Times* then would not have covered Mick Jagger's divorce or David Beckham's personal life. The only broadsheet or former broadsheet that does not cover this sort of thing now is the *Financial Times*. The tabloids are of course full of stories about the ordinary everyday doings of TV personalities.

ELITE NATIONS

More news stories will be written about political developments in elite nations, particularly the US, because the political developments of these nations affect us all more than developments in, say, Spain. This was clear during the recent Iraq war. But it is also true to say that more human interest stories emanate from elite nations. The ongoing debate about gun laws in the US, or the facts about obesity among American children, are both covered more than similar stories would be, say, from Italy. There may be many reasons for this. We already hear about US politics because they are important (see above), so we are ready to hear more about their lifestyle. Most Europeans probably know a few US citizens personally, and we feel we know even more of them because we know about American film and music stars. Many of us have been to the US on holiday. Also, there are simply more foreign correspondents reporting what is going on there.

NEGATIVITY

Bad news makes more interesting stories than good news. In my view this is true only because bad news fits more of the rest of the criteria above, such as unexpectedness. If we all have jobs, earn a reasonable amount of money, have parties from time to time, and go on holiday, then none of that is newsworthy. But if our house burns down it is news. If really good things happen to people unexpectedly (rediscovering a long-lost child, finding a Rembrandt in the attic) then that does make big news. So I think the bad news point derives from the fact that bad news is generally unexpected, and affects people's lives.

CONTINUITY

Once a story has been covered, it is likely to be covered some more. Some aspects of this are pretty obvious: if there has been a big political event, such as a government defeat in the House of Commons, then there will be more developments in the days that follow, and so these will be covered. There is another point about this though, which is that if one slightly odd event happens and is covered in the press, then another similar event will get more coverage. Let's say a small child is attacked by a Jack Russell terrier. If a few days later another Jack Russell attacks another child, the second story will be given more prominence. If this happens a third time there will be big coverage, interviews with animal behaviourists, calls for action in Parliament, and so on.

UNAMBIGUITY

This means that to get on to the news list, the story needs to be easily understood. The theory is that sudden dramatic events are more likely to be covered than a lengthy argument about policy changes. I am not so sure

I agree with this. Reporters on nationals, and on B2B (trade) magazines, are experts in their particular specialisms, and generally watch carefully what is going on in that field. Even in a complicated long-running story, they home in on a new announcement, or a leak of a change of plan, and use that as a starting point for a story.

MEANINGFULNESS

This is generally interpreted as meaning that people like to read about people like themselves. I guess this is true, if only because people like ourselves are doing the same things that we are doing. You probably wouldn't get a story about viewing figures for *Big Brother* in Ghana.

CONSONANCE

This means that a story needs to fit with what the readers expect. I am not too sure about this one either. It seems to me to be almost the opposite of the 'unexpectedness' category above. If John Prescott bought a very big new car, it would get into the news because it is what we expect. But if he bought a scooter it would get into the news as well. It is certainly the case that readers want, or papers believe that readers want, to be told things that suit their existing prejudices. A paper might run a number of stories that are critical of the European Union because that is what the editors believe the readers want to hear.

CRITERIA RELATING TO THE TREATMENT OF NEWS

COMPOSITION

Stories get into the news for all the reasons in this list, but they also get in to give a balance. If a newspaper covers one grisly murder trial in detail, it might cover another one in rather less detail. *Private Eye* often makes jokes in brackets on the lines of: 'That's enough grisly murders – ed'. Most papers like a good solid human-interest story on page three. They might put a dramatic trial story there, but quite often it will be a story about the new Dr Who, or J. K. Rowling's earnings. This is especially so at the weekend, when there is a feeling that most readers, who are having a relaxing start to their day, want something jolly to read early on in the paper.

Part of this same point is the fact that a story might get into a newspaper or magazine because there is a very good photo to go with it. Without the photo the story might be spiked. The same is particularly true of television reporting. Stories get in because there is a dramatic bit of film to go with them, and without that dramatic film, the story will be spiked.

PERSONALIZATION

This means seeing stories in terms of people. This again seems to me to be a point about how news is covered. Politics is often seen as a clash between individual party leaders rather than between the parties, but this seems to be a style of reporting. It was very noticeable during the recent Iraq war that much of the coverage focused on stories about individuals. This is often the way news is reported now, and it is very different from the way it was done 50 years ago. The fact remains though, that it is the political clash, or the conflict in Iraq itself, which is the essence of the news: the personalization is simply a way of illustrating that story.

Sarah Niblock cites two other criteria which are important but are not included in Galtung and Ruge:

EXCLUSIVITY

A newspaper or magazine will give great prominence to a story which it believes that no rivals have got. Of course, the story will fit several of the other criteria, but its exclusivity will be a major factor in the kind of display it gets, and whether other stories are left out of the paper.

Newspapers go to enormous lengths to make sure that an exclusive story is just that. When *The Times* had all to itself the story about Edwina Currie's revelations of her affair with John Major, many of the most senior journalists in the office that day were not told about it. Secretly, away from the main news floor, a double-page spread was prepared with extracts from the Currie book and all the details. The first editions of newspapers are delivered to all the other newspaper offices in London towards the end of the evening, and other papers would have had time to get something in if they had seen the story in the first edition. So the story was left out of the first edition, and the spread filled with a huge double-page advert, simply slotted in to fill the paper. And what was the ad? For Currys.

CONFLICT

This is intrinsic to some of the other criteria. It is easy to see in such areas as international relations and politics, but as I shall show, a great deal of news is related to the disagreements and conflicts within a situation, in a row about a football transfer, or a council planning decision.

CASE STUDY: WHAT MAKES A STORY NEWSWORTHY

This brings me neatly to my own theories of news values. Syma Tariq, a former student, and I collated every news story in the British national papers for two days in July 2005 and classified them. We excluded all the stories in the business sections, not because they were not newsworthy, but because they form a specialized group of stories and in a way are more like the stories in a B2B publication. For the same reason, we excluded the *Financial Times* entirely, because although it is a national paper, it has elements of a specialized local paper, with very different news values.

For the same reason, we excluded all the sports stories. Again, the sports sections are the equivalent of a local paper or B2B magazine, with many stories which fit with some of the criteria for news selection, but they are mainly there because a specialized audience wants lots of details about past or future sporting events.

The dates we chose, in the middle of July, were busy news days, partly because of the aftermath of the July 7 bomb attacks in London. We took every story and tried to work out the main reason for its inclusion in the paper. Of course, most stories are published for several different reasons, but we decided to focus on what appeared to be the main one, to try to identify the categories which stories fit into. We ended up with six broad categories:

- Conflict
- Celebrities
- Human interest: relevance to me the reader
- Human interest: ordinary people
- Quirks
- Science/research and discovery

I shall take each category in turn.

CONFLICT

Within this heading we grouped four subheadings, which are all, in my view, related to conflict and/or drama:

- Actual conflict
- Politics
- Crime
- Natural disasters and accidents

Stories about *actual conflicts*, in July 2005, formed by far the biggest category. There were many stories in the papers about the aftermath of the London attacks, generally about eight or so in each of the broadsheets or former broadsheets. There were stories from Iraq and Afghanistan, although these stories were far fewer, pushed out probably by the London stories. Then there were stories about other conflicts, for example in Sri Lanka, Indonesia, Thailand and Guatemala.

Stories about *politics* formed the second biggest subgroup. In a democracy, politics is about conflict in its broadest sense: it is a discussion/debate/argument about the best way to organize society, how much tax should be raised, what it should be spent on, what is the best way to improve hospitals or schools and so on. The stories in politics come from those arguments, those tensions between two or more possibilities. In a dictatorship there would be far fewer political stories, simply because there would not be that kind of argument between the two or more sides. On our two days there were stories about the figures for asylum seekers, payments to troublesome teenagers, the Conservative Party leadership election, plans for more housing, and many more. All of them were based on some sort of tension, or argument, implied or otherwise, between different groups.

Stories about *crime* formed another big subgroup. Crime stories, whether about the original crime, or the court case that might follow, are also all about conflict and drama. Violence is obviously conflict, but so is burglary or robbery: it is a conflict between the mugger and the mugged for possession of the purse or jewellery. The reports of a court case have several levels of conflict: the conflict in the original crime, and the conflict in the court proceedings itself; the arguments about whether or not the accused actually committed the crime, and about the likely punishment.

We fitted *natural disasters* into the conflict category as well: they are in a sense a conflict between different elements on Earth: between rivers and their banks, or between the Earth and its crust. The most dramatic stories happen of course when large numbers of people become caught up in the conflict. I decided that *accidents* also fitted into this category: in the broadest sense an accident is a conflict between two vehicles, or a vehicle and a tree, or a person and a river.

CELEBRITIES

Galtung and Ruge called this category 'elite people', but celebs is certainly what we call them today. It is fascinating to collate every celeb story in all the newspapers, to see the huge variety of stories and, it must be said, the inconsequential nature of so many of them.

With the conflict and political stories, and to a certain extent the other groupings, many of the papers have the same three or four stories, with perhaps a couple of extra ones which are carried in only a couple of the papers. But the list of celeb stories in the tabloids is enormous, and enormously varied. Many of the stories fit into other categories as well, but we put them in the celeb category if it seemed that the story was there mainly because it was about the famous person. So we included stories that had elements of conflict, such as court cases involving celebs, if we felt that the story would not have got into the paper without the famous name.

The fascinating thing is that the tabloids have all got the same main stories, such as lots of stories about *Celebrity Big Brother* and the Jude Law/ nanny story. But then they have in many cases completely different sets of secondary celeb stories, with whole pages devoted to different minor stories, in many cases about pretty minor people. This is probably partly because the papers have these stories about minor celebs as exclusives, and indeed the other papers may well follow up the same stories later in the week. Seeing the main point of the stories written out does bring home how tiny some of these stories are:

Jessica Alba kisses a monkey
Coleen has parking row
Beckham shaves armpits

For these and plenty of others, it is clear that it is *only* the name that makes the news; there is no other news point at all in many of them.

The other interesting thing about the celeb stories is how many are covered in the broadsheets or former broadsheets. The Jude Law story, which had been broken on the Sunday, was heavily covered in all the tabloids on Monday. The story for them was the fact of his affair, plus reaction. *The Times* gave it one paragraph, based on his public apology, presumably on the grounds that it does not report affairs but can report a public statement. The *Daily Telegraph* and the *Guardian* both got into it in quite a big way the next day, with photographs and more detail, and all the tabloids carried new stories on July 19 as well. Only the *Independent* ignored the story entirely.

Another interesting story was about the film director Roman Polanski testifying by video link in a libel case against *Vanity Fair*. This was covered in detail by the broadsheets and compacts, but ignored entirely by the *Sun* and the *Daily Star*. The case turned on allegations of a sexual adventure in 1969, so perhaps these two papers decided that the whole thing simply happened too long ago to interest their readers.

We fitted some other slightly random stories into this category. The *Guardian* ran a great story based on newly released files from Special Branch, which showed that they had watched and reported on the writer George Orwell for 12 years. So Big Brother really was watching him, just as his character Winston Smith was watched in his novel *1984*. Other papers did not carry this, perhaps because their reporters did not spot it when the documents were released. It certainly was an excellent story for the left-leaning *Guardian*.

HUMAN INTEREST: RELEVANCE TO THE READER

In our survey, we put into this group all the stories that we felt people would read because they had some relevance to their own lives. So stories about taxation, house prices, forecasts of a heatwave and all the many different health stories, fitted into this category. People are interested in them because they have relevance to their own health, or the price of their house, or the way these things affect family members or friends. Then we also included all the various survey stories, since we decided that the interest of these stories lay in how people would relate them to their own experience:

> Wine drinkers are slimmer/healthier/cleverer than those who drink beer and spirits
> Pensioners are more likely to spend money than leave any inheritance
> Britons like sex on holiday
> Women spend an average of £31,000 on shoes in a lifetime
> Ready-made salads are too salty

Again it is very noticeable that while several papers covered two or three of the main stories, different papers carried several which few others carried.

The *Independent*, as it is now in the habit of doing, ran a big story which no other paper covered, about the possibility of drought. The front page was almost entirely taken up with a picture of dried-up mud in a reservoir near East Grinstead. The back-up story was a 'worked up' one, with no particular news point other than that the editor had decided to give us an update on the dwindling water supply.

The *Guardian* was the only one to go for

> Women getting rich faster than men

based on a report from a bank. It was worked up into a page lead with a picture of a successful woman, and a profile/interview sidebar. It looked to me like a good story for the *Daily Mail*, or indeed the *Daily Telegraph*, but maybe these papers just didn't get around to it.

As one might have expected, only the *Sun* and the *Daily Star* ran

> Women bare 50 per cent more flesh than a decade ago

while *The Times* had several stories that other papers did not run, including

Drivers want more traffic police
Libraries risk becoming relics

The *Daily Telegraph*, with a large country readership, went for

Countryside under threat in Prescott homes plan
Sheep dip wipes out insect river life

We included one almost indefinable story in this group:

London Zoo to get rid of cages

which ran in *The Times,* the *Guardian* and the *Daily Mirror*. It seemed that in the end this story would strike a chord in terms of the reader's experience: either having been to London Zoo and not been happy about the cages, or having been and not minded.

We also fitted the various stories about the BBC into this category: they included stories about promises of fewer repeats, of possible moves to Manchester and so on. It seemed to us that the BBC interests us because we are probably all consumers, and because we all pay the licence fee, so its plans affect us all.

Many of these stories have elements of conflict in them too. In fact the best ones almost always do: an education story for example, which is also part of a political disagreement.

HUMAN INTEREST: ORDINARY PEOPLE

This turned out to embrace a rather smaller number of stories than we expected. We put into this group those stories that were primarily about unusual things happening to ordinary people. They included dramatic human tragedies, such as a couple committing suicide after the suicide of their only son, and a British climber dying in a fall in the Alps. But there were other less tragic stories too:

Poker player wins $7.5 million in World Series Poker
Woman passes driving test after 33 years

We used this category for stories that were simply about interesting things happening to people. Again, plenty of these 'ordinary life' stories involve conflict or drama, especially the more tragic ones. With the more jokey ones, there is often some overlap with the next category.

QUIRKS

Agencies used to use the term 'quirk' for a strange little story which has no significance, is not relevant to any reader's life or experience, but is simply peculiar. It seems to me a perfect word to describe all the off-beat little stories which get into the papers. The animal stories that papers are fond of including in their **nibs** (news in briefs) columns often fit into this category.

There were lots of quirks during July 18/19. Every paper carried a picture and story about an art installation in Newcastle by the New York artist Spencer Tunick, who specializes in large installations of naked people. It was a gift to the papers to make a jolly page among lots of other gloomy stories. The broadsheets and compacts mostly went for fairly tasteful shots, especially one that showed most of the participants from the back. The *Sun*, however, managed to get a full frontal shot of three girls, and then superimposed in strategic positions images of the Gateshead Angel of the North sculpture.

Several carried a story about laughing gas (nitrous oxide) producing the best bubbles in Aero chocolate, another about London pigeons getting fatter because of the huge amounts of fast food left lying about, and delays to rail services caused by a stray cow on the line. There was a swan which attacked a man during the annual Thames swan upping, a panda caught in a tree, a village plagued by peacocks, and snail-racing championships.

SCIENCE/RESEARCH AND DISCOVERY

The last, rather small, category perhaps overlaps with the quirks a little, since some of the research, discovery and invention stories are very off-beat. Both *The Times* and the *Guardian* had a great story about researchers discovering a shift in the gene pool of elephants in China. More are being born without tusks, because this makes them less likely to be shot by poachers.

Several papers carried a story about how scientists have discovered that flies escape from being swatted by jumping rather than flying away. Of course, as we have seen, every story has more than one element in it, and this one has some conflict and drama, at least for the fly. Archaeological and historical discoveries fit into this category as well, such as

Silver from Pompeii's ashes displayed

SO HOW DO YOU SPOT AND DEVELOP A NEWS STORY?

When I talk about this to students, we make a big Venn diagram on the board, and slot the day's stories into it. There are two side groups, *discovery* and *quirks*, which are more or less separate from all the rest. But the vast majority of the stories that appear on the news pages of every paper, fit into the broad categories of *conflict/drama* and/or *people*. Most stories of course have elements of both (see Figure 1).

So these elements are what you need to look for when you are working out whether you have got a good story, and what exactly that story is:

- Where is the conflict/tension/argument or drama?
- And where are the people?

The people could be either the people involved, or the people affected, or both. The best stories will have both these elements in them, and that is what the reporter needs to bring out.

The very best story of course will include conflict and drama, be about a famous person, and be relevant to the reader, and have a good picture to go with it. So if Jude Law confronts the government about cutting taxes, while being photographed with a new starlet, we're there.

Years ago some friends on a local paper spent some time constructing the perfect headline (the story, unfortunately, has yet to happen):

Duke's Son Weeps In Helicopter Rape Court Drama

Finally, it is worth noting that the groups of stories we decided early on not to consider, do fit into this broad category of conflict. All sport is about conflict and drama – 22 people arguing about which direction a ball should go in, or a few people disputing which of them can get round a track before the others. And business stories in the popular papers are very much about celebs, in the sense that these papers cover Manchester United, Marks & Spencer and other famous organizations. The business stories in the broadsheets and compacts are often about conflict and drama such as hostile takeovers.

Those stories that have less conflict in them often fit into the 'relevance to the reader category' because the readers need to know the doings of firms or markets in which they are investing.

The big balloon on the left represents all the stories with an element of conflict. The one of the right represents all the stories which are about people, with celebrities towards the top of the balloon, stories which are

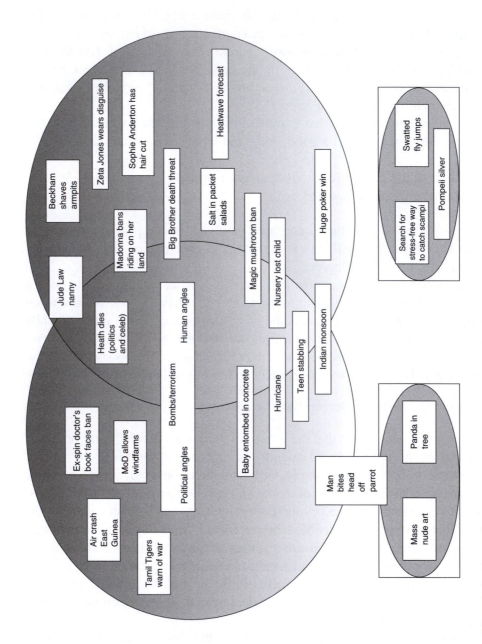

Figure 1   What makes news?

relevant to the readers' own lives in the middle, and ordinary people/human interest towards the bottom. Then where the two overlap are the stories which are about celebs involved in conflict, or further down, conflict and drama which affect us and further down still, conflict and drama affecting ordinary people.

The small balloon lower left includes quirks, and the one on the right science, research and discovery.

GATHERING THE NEWS

NEWS SOURCES

News stories arise from things that happen which are of interest to your readership. Many of these are actual events, from burst water mains or road crashes to horse shows and school plays.

Very often the reporter witnesses the event because it was expected (courts, meetings, football matches, demonstrations): the event has been on the news-desk diary, and the reporter has been sent to cover it. These are known as diary stories. Other types of story, often the best ones, are about something that was entirely unforeseen. In these cases, the reporter gets information from others who witnessed it, or who for some reason know about it (police, fire officers). Sometimes reporters are 'lucky' enough to be present when something dramatic happens. Lucky of course is not always the right word – a recent example is that of the journalists who were on holiday in Thailand on December 26 2004.

In a great many cases, the 'thing that happened' is simply something that someone has said, and her words become news because of her position and/or what she said. News stories based on what people say arise in several ways. A newsworthy person might speak at a public or private event of some sort, or she might speak to a reporter in an interview, either face to face or on the phone, or she might produce a document and make it available. Sometimes she might produce a document and not make it available. If this document gets into the reporter's hands, it can make a very good story.

Another distinct category is stories which the reporter originates. Reporters describe these as **off-diary** stories, or stories they have brought in. Reporters find these by talking to **contacts**, or simply through observing what is going on around them.

Quotes from people are essential to all new stories, whether they are about a major dramatic event such as a disaster, or an announcement about a council decision. Quotes bring the story to life, highlight the tensions between groups of people, tell us exactly what happened, explain its significance, paint a picture, and tell us what might happen next. Listening and/or talking to people and recording what they say form the backbone of a reporter's job.

THE REPORTER'S NOTEBOOK

I urge students always to use a spiral-bound reporter's notebook, and to rule a margin down the side of each page before beginning to report. Use this margin to put stars or squiggles against quotes that you think might be important, or to make notes to check names or other facts.

Put your name on it, and date the notebook on the front with the first day it was used. Write *everything* in it: the date, name and place of an event before you go to it, or the name of the interviewee before you talk to her (and check with her that you have got it right). Obviously write down what happened, but write down everything else that might be important, from the name of the news editor when you start a new job, to the name of the pub which someone recommends. Write down the address of the office you are working in! I knew a reporter years ago, before the days of mobile phones, who was sent out on a job on her first day at a new paper, but then couldn't get back to the office to report it because she couldn't remember where the office was.

When you have used up the notebook, add to the front the last date that something was written in it, and keep it for a couple of years. There have been plenty of cases where an interviewee or an official has denied saying something. The more organized your notebooks are, the more likely you are to be able to retrieve the correct quote. It also looks tremendously efficient and impressive if the editor calls you in to question you about your notes. If there is a dispute about your reporting, careful and well-organized notes may help you to prove that you have reported someone accurately and this might prevent you from getting fired.

It is a slog to learn shorthand, and Britain is the only country where it is very highly regarded, but the fact is that an accurate shorthand note of something regularly saves a reporter's job when a story is challenged. In 1999 Matt Dickinson of *The Times* interviewed Glenn Hoddle, the then England football manager, and reported him as saying he believed that people were born with disabilities because of a karma from a previous life. There was a fantastic row, and Hoddle vehemently denied having said this. Dickinson was able to show his editor his notebook with a clear note of what had been said. Dickinson kept his job and Hoddle lost his.

Let's look at the main sources of news in turn. They are:

1 Events
2 Written material
3 Ideas originated by the reporter

EVENTS

Most of these are events at which the reporter is a witness, though there are some at which the reporter is a participant, such as press conferences. They include:

- Meetings
- Courts
- Sporting events of every sort
- Theatrical and other performances, displays, parades, demonstrations

Certain things about all these different events make them easy to report. But there are plenty of things that make them difficult as well. On the plus side, there will actually *be* a news story. On the minus side, it can be difficult to work out what is going on, which councillor is on which side, which group a lawyer is representing. It may be difficult to collect all the information needed for a good story, and it is very common for an inexperienced reporter to get back the office after the event is over, only to find that she hasn't got enough material to make a coherent news story.

MEETINGS

These include sittings of every kind of political forum, from parliament to parish councils; meetings of other groups such as health authorities or planning inquiries; protest meetings and other pressure group events.

National and local politicians, health authorities and similar bodies make decisions all the time which affect people's lives, so they are bound to become news stories in the 'relevance to the reader' category. They may also provide some sort of conflict, if the politicians cannot agree on the best way forward.

Since the executive system was introduced, reporting council meetings has become much more difficult. It is much rarer nowadays to be sitting in a meeting when a dramatic decision is taken, such as closing a care home or building a new school. But there are still some set-piece newsworthy events, such as planning inquiries and licensing committees.

It is essential to prepare well before going to the event, making sure you get all the background information you possibly can before you set off. With council meetings, pressure groups and planning inquiries, there are likely to be papers available beforehand, such as agenda, reports, statements from various parties and so on. The more you can find out beforehand, especially about what is likely to happen, the more likely you are to spot if something unexpected, and therefore newsworthy, happens. Make sure you have a list of the participants, with correct spellings, titles and positions in their organization.

Print out lists of councillors with mugshots from the internet. See if you can work out which other people might be there. If a church is protesting about a nearby development for example, there will probably be a picture of the vicar on the internet so you can work out who he is beforehand.

Get to the event early, talk to anyone who seems to know what is going on, try to work out at least a few of the names of the people who are likely to speak. But if you haven't got all the names before things start, don't waste time worrying about that and risk missing a good quote. Get the quote down and put beside it 'fat lawyer' or 'bearded Lib Dem' or 'red shirt'. You will have time to sort out afterwards who is who, but you will have forgotten the quote if you haven't got it down.

Take a licensing committee meeting considering a late music licence for a local club. You will get the facts in the committee agenda, where the club is and so on. You will probably get on paper the main points from any protesters, and they will have more to say at the meeting. You will get the club's side from its manager or other representative. You wait around for a bit, and get the result. Apart from a few extra quotes perhaps, the story is there.

After the event, if necessary, you can approach people to check things, especially after political or protest meetings. Generally both sides will want their names and details correct in the paper so they will be willing to help.

COURTS

Covering these forms a large part of many reporters' daily work. They range from magistrates' courts and inquests to crown courts, appeal courts, civil courts and extradition hearings. Increasingly, local papers are ignoring magistrates' courts. You can sit there for hours listening to motoring and shoplifting cases which are not that interesting. There are often delays because the accused and/or the witnesses don't turn up. There might be a case which sounds quite newsworthy, but then it turns out that the person in the dock is not from your area and so your news editor won't be interested.

Many local papers are finding that they can get better human interest stories in other ways. Often, especially in big cities, court reporting is done by agencies, whose reporters spend most of their time at one or two courts. They get to know all the officials and often some of the lawyers, and so they find it easier to keep tabs on which cases are coming up, and which will provide the best stories. The agencies can then sell stories aimed at different audiences to various papers all round the city.

Remember when reporting courts that while justice must be seen to be done, and reporters are entitled to be there, in some cases you are likely to be tolerated rather than welcomed. So dress smartly, turn your mobile phone off and keep quiet.

Criminal court cases can be newsworthy in two ways. The events that led to the case are often newsworthy, since crime always involves some sort of conflict. And there is another possibility of conflict and drama at the court hearing itself, with one side trying to prove something and another side denying it. The number of TV plays based on court proceedings shows this.

Inquests do not always have a great deal of intrinsic conflict. They are investigative, they are about finding out what happened, not about apportioning blame. In theory an inquest is not intended to be a forum where two sides with opposing views seek to show that their own view is correct. Having said that, some inquests do take on this character, when for example a family is unhappy about the treatment a relative had in hospital or in prison. But even without that conflict, inquests almost always make a story, because the simple fact that there is an inquest means that the death was unexpected. News stories are generally about the unexpected rather than the run-of-the-mill.

It is similar with a crown court case. Since crime is generally dramatic, there is no difficulty about working out what the story is. If you are in court long enough, and take careful notes, you will get enough to make a good story. It might be difficult, in a long and complicated case, to order all the material into a good news story, but there is no doubt that the material will be there.

If you have to check things, do so politely afterwards. Inquests and other court cases are traumatic for those involved, and you need to be particularly careful to avoid being ghoulish. Inexperienced reporters obviously need to be very careful about approaching either families at inquests, or families of accused people in court cases. But if you are brief and discreet, people sometimes don't mind.

I don't let gaggles of students approach people after court cases, but once after an inquest I talked to a friend of the dead man. We had heard in court that he was a well-known performer in local pubs and clubs, and he had collapsed on stage. What we didn't hear, as I discovered from the friend, was that he was a drag artist, with a stage name which had not come out at the inquest. He was well known locally by this stage name, but not known at all by his real name. This information gave the story a completely different angle.

If you are being sent to cover a particular court case, get any details from the **cuttings** about the crime or sudden death. This is often difficult, but any information beforehand will make things a bit easier when you get there: what the crime was, when and where it took place. Always have an A–Z with you to check places and areas. Don't leave without getting all the information you need. It is well nigh impossible to check anything about a court case afterwards, court officials are busy people and don't have much time to spare to help junior reporters, and they certainly won't help on the phone the next day. So if the place name you hear in court is not the same as in the cutting you have from the paper at the time of the crime, check it with someone before you leave.

It is a very good idea to make a checklist of points you must get: who, what, when, where and so on. It sounds a bit obvious, but I have seen plenty of students come away from an inquest without being absolutely certain of, say, where the death occurred. During the actual case, your main focus should be on getting good accurate quotes, so get them down against the word 'neighbour' or 'driver'. But then make sure you check the details in the recess or after the case. You must get the name somehow, if you want to quote someone.

This brings me to a specific point about court reporting. Everything should be sourced in a court report, so don't end up with any substantive points which are not pinned onto a witness. Of course you don't have to write 'Mrs Jones said' in every paragraph, but take care that anyone reading your final version can be in no doubt where each of the main points came from. Any good news editor will insist on this, because it gives weight to every point, and is important if there were to be a dispute or complaint about the story.

Beware of getting extra material or quotes outside the court. Learn the laws of libel and contempt thoroughly from one of the media law books. Suffice to say that with the main exception of cases involving children, anything said in court can be reported, so long as the reporting is accurate and timely. However, if there is controversy about a death in police custody for example, a reporter needs to be very careful if using extra remarks that were not made in court.

SPORTING EVENTS

Research beforehand. Find out who is playing! Get team lists, find out what the teams have been doing recently. Find out what happened when they last met, who is expected to win, etc. Then if there is an unexpected upset, you can immediately see what the story is. The peculiar thing about sports reporting is that very often large numbers of the potential readers have also seen the match. So you need to keep your wits about you the whole time, because if you say X made the match-winning pass when it was actually made by Y, your readers will not forgive you.

There is often a chance to talk to players, coaches and officials after the game, and indeed the post-match press conference can make up a large part of the story. You will get better quotes at this if you were clear what was expected to happen, and if there was any upset.

Sports reporters often have to work at tremendous speed. Sports results and reports are vital for newspapers, especially the tabloids, whose edition timings and distribution are often dictated by sporting events. Reporters sometimes have to write some of the match report on the way *to* the game and then slot in a couple of paragraphs at the top about the result.

THEATRICAL AND OTHER PERFORMANCES, PARADES AND DISPLAYS

These are often rather soft in terms of news, especially if everything goes according to plan. So again, research beforehand, find out what is different about this event: first time at this venue, celeb in the cast, bigger crowd expected, new songs specially written. Again, the more preparation you can do beforehand, the better your story will be, because you will be able to get more relevant quotes. But be prepared for the fact that the story might change in the light of events. No one will care so much about the new songs if the roof of the stage collapses.

There was a lovely example a few years ago of a BBC Promenade concert at the Albert Hall, when at the last minute the soprano could not sing. An appeal went out to the audience: 'Can anyone sing this role?' A music student said she could, and did so. At least one national newspaper carried a straight review of the concert the next day, with a line at the end: 'XX, who stepped into the role of Violetta at the last minute, gave a good account.' Once the papers woke up to what had happened, the story was all over them, with pictures of the young student outside the Albert Hall, and lots of quotes.

The main problem with reporting all live events such as these is that you may get only one chance to spot the best news angle. If you are reading a document looking for a news point, you can pore over it and read it through several times working out what is the best angle. You can mark paragraphs, think about whether what they contain is new, check background either on the internet or with officials, and so on. When you are witnessing a live event you haven't got this luxury, you need to spot the news as you go along. If you are working for an evening paper, you may not have time to go carefully through the many pages of notes from a three-hour court case. You have to mark a couple of good quotes, get the facts right, and be able to write it in time for the next edition.

Accuracy is essential of course. It is essential because your editor will want the events correctly reported, the names right and so on. In court cases it is also essential because the privilege to report allegations that would otherwise be libellous ('that man attacked me with a crowbar') is extended only if your reporting is accurate (see the various handbooks on media law).

STORIES FROM WRITTEN MATERIAL

Many different kinds of written material make news stories. The most obvious ones are of course **press releases**. These are documents usually written by press officers within an organization specifically with the intention of getting the information reported in the press.

The most junior reporter is often assigned to look through press releases. All government groups, political parties, pressure groups, businesses, religious organizations, theatres, etc. produce press releases. Generally, though not always, a press release will have some sort of news point, and depending on how good the press officers are, it will be easy to spot. But of course the author of the release is going to try to show her own organization in the best possible light, so press releases demand a critical eye to ensure that you are not falling for a particular line from a council or other group.

If time permits, most news editors would want the reporter to make a couple of calls on a press release. This is so that your paper gets a slightly different quote from the one on the document, and therefore ends up with a slightly different story from your rival's.

Then there are all the other kinds of political document, from government bills, white and green papers, down to local council agendas, reports and planning applications. Health authorities and other official bodies such as Transport for London publish reports. There are annual reports from companies, and reports and other documents from pressure groups and charities.

Reporting from some of these is generally rather harder, and takes a bit of experience.

Good reporters develop a knack of spotting a story in some apparently unpromising reports and charts. Some students of mine were assigned to look through the reports and statistics for a council social services committee. They included lots of tables and facts about children in care homes in the borough and what they thought about the care they were receiving. One student winkled out the following fact: under the column 'birthday celebrated?' nearly half the children questioned said their birthdays had not been marked. Assuming this was true, it was a very good local story, possibly even a good idea for a Sunday national, and it was not spotted by any of the local papers.

STORIES ORIGINATED BY THE REPORTER

These fall into two broad categories. There are stories from contacts and 'off-diary' stories.

STORIES FROM CONTACTS

Even the smallest publication tends to get its reporters to specialize in one area. Often on a local paper, reporters are expected to cover particular fields such as education, council or crime. These are generally known in Britain as the reporter's specialism, or in the US, her beat. Reporters on local papers are also often assigned to a geographical patch.

The reporter is expected to get to know some of the people living in the area, or involved in the issue (contacts), to find out what is going on, what is likely to happen and why, and so on. That specialist knowledge means that the reporter can come up with possible stories, see angles, and perhaps persuade contacts to give advance information so that her paper gets a story before the opposition. The more contacts are cultivated, the more stories the reporter will get.

OFF-DIARY STORIES

This expression means just that: stories the reporter gets which did not appear on the newsdesk diary. Off-diary work is particularly important on local papers.

At City University we have a long tradition of sending students out to a specific small area of London and telling them not to come back until they have found two stories. It is pretty scary the first time, and plenty of the students' hearts must sink as they wander out armed only with a notebook. The first time they do it, it is hard to convince them that they will get anything. But more often than not they come up with excellent stories after a couple of hours of scanning an area. Some of the stories of course would be known to a reporter covering that patch, but even so, it proves that there are stories all over the place if you only know where to look. In one trawl of the Covent Garden area, students came up with:

- Fears about a possible big redevelopment altering the character of the area
- The then new phenomenon of people with sandwich boards pointing tourists to burger bars
- The symbiotic relationship between a new film and a chain of fashion stores – the stores advertised the film, the film 'product placed' the stores
- A new poetry café
- The (admittedly perennial) problems of the rickshaw cyclists

The point about off-diary work is that a reporter needs to develop two important skills: first the ability to notice when anything has changed, and whether the change might be a story, and second the ability to talk to anyone and everyone. It can be hard for young students or trainees to get talking to people they don't know. The answer to that is to practise. Get used to saying something, anything, to everyone you meet. Most people don't mind this at all, in fact assistants in corner shops and supermarket checkouts generally welcome it: by making conversation you are treating them as people. If all else fails, talk about the weather, and then move on to talking about the food in a café, the road works outside, anything. The more you can be at ease talking to different kinds of people, the better your interviewing skills will be.

Off-diary stories are bottom-up rather than top-down. If reporters get plenty of off-diary stories it means that as well as reporting the doings of the council and other bodies from the point of view of those organizations, the paper gets stories that have started with ordinary people and local issues.

OTHER SOURCES OF NEWS

The main ones are:

- Rival publications, to see whether they got something which you missed, and which you could therefore follow up

- Local radio and TV
- National newspapers, radio and TV, to see what national stories can be developed using a local angle
- Advertisements: in publications, radio, local cinema, shop windows, fly posters, leaflets
- Last but not least: the internet. Students are so adept at finding material on the internet that it can be difficult to persuade them that there is anywhere else to look. That is why we like sending them out to find off-diary stories. But is it true that a lot of off-beat stories can be found on the internet.

GETTING THE RIGHT QUOTE

Other books deal in detail with interviewing of all kinds. But it is worth saying here that you won't get a good news story written if you have not got the right quotes. It is important to be proactive, whether simply listening in a court or talking to someone on the phone. A good reporter homes in on the drama and conflict in a story, and makes sure she records the quotes that will highlight that drama and conflict. If there has been a dramatic event, the good reporter will picture the event, and make sure she records the quotes which will give the reader the best picture.

If possible, before speaking to someone, think ahead to what the main point of the story might be, and make sure you get the right quote to back that up. It is important of course not to be so certain of what you think is the main story that you miss another interesting and unforeseen angle that emerges. But it is vital to know what kind of quote from your subjects will bring the story to life and make sure you give the subject an opportunity to give you that quote.

THE INTRO

The first sentence of a news story is known as the intro, short for introduction. It is almost always written as a paragraph on its own. In news stories the paragraphs almost never follow the rules for paragraphs in essay-writing. Because most news stories, even in magazines, are laid out in fairly narrow columns, paragraphs are usually made up of one or two sentences. Short paragraphs are easier to read quickly, and speed is what it is all about. It is worth getting into the habit of breaking your story up into very short paragraphs. It is best to do this partly because the copy will have to be broken up when it goes into a page in a magazine or newspaper, but also because it helps you to see if you have made some sentences too long and therefore hard to follow.

The cliché that today's newspaper is tomorrow's fish wrapper may not be literally true any more, but the fact is that readers have not paid much for their papers (in many cases they have paid nothing) and their interest has to be won every time by the writer, and by the page designers and headline writers.

Theorists have discussed different kinds of writing, and how some writing has to be read, some is read for pleasure and so on. A novelist can take longer than a news reporter to draw a reader in. Several friends may have told the reader how great the book is, there may have been a great deal of publicity, and the reader has probably spent £10 or more on it, so she is at least going to invest an hour or two in seeing if it is worth reading. Similarly, plenty of other types of writing do not need to win the reader over with every new sentence: a form explaining how to obtain a passport doesn't have to be especially interesting, because the reader has got to read it to find out what to do.

None of this applies to a news story. The reader has paid nothing, or next to nothing for it, and unfortunately values it accordingly. So the story has to engage the reader from beginning to end. The first sentence has to persuade your reader to read the second, the second has to persuade her to read the third, and so on.

A reporter writing a classic news story, of the type which appears in newspapers, magazines and on agency services every day, aims to grab the reader's attention by putting the most important and interesting point first. The idea is that this event will be so interesting that the reader will be prepared to invest another couple of seconds in reading the second paragraph, and so on. This diminishing order of importance, set out in a diagrammatic way in the inverted pyramid, is set out in more detail in Chapter 4.

The second good reason for telling the most important fact at the beginning is in a way the opposite of the first reason. It is that if the most important thing is in the first sentence, readers can move on to another story safe in the knowledge that they do at least know the main piece of news in the first story. Agencies adopt this principle so that their subscribers, newspapers, magazines, radio and TV stations, can immediately tell the value of the story.

In a classic news story the first paragraph seeks to answer the question 'What happened?' The way this is often taught in colleges and training courses is by reference to the five Ws.

THE FIVE WS

These are:

Who?
What?
When?
Where?
Why?

Trainees at Reuters are told about the Six Ws, the sixth being hoW? In my view, How? might be part of the What happened? Or it might be part of the Why? answer.

Reuters also insists that there is a **source** in the first paragraph. The agency considers it essential that subscribers can judge the worth of a story immediately by assessing where it has come from. This is certainly one of the reasons for the strength of the agency's reputation for accuracy and reliability, though it can occasionally lead to slightly unusual intros. When the US embassy hostages, who had been held in Iran for 444 days, were finally released in 1981, the story on the Reuters wire went something like:

> The aircraft carrying the US hostages took off from Iranian soil today, a Reuters reporter at the scene said.

It may have looked slightly odd, but for subscribers in the United States it was essential to make clear that this event had actually happened, and been witnessed by a reliable source. You should always work out whether you need a source in the intro. If there is likely to be any doubt in your reader's mind that the story might be true, it would be worth including a source.

It will not always be possible or necessary to include the answers to all five W questions in the first sentence, but it is always a good idea to check off all five, and either make sure you have answered them, or have satisfied yourself that one or two of the answers can be left until further down the story. Let's look at each of the five Ws separately.

WHO?

This will nearly always be a person or group of people:

> Tony Blair hit out at critics last night …
> Twenty people were injured when a tornado …

Thinking back to Chapter 1, news stories are about people and/or conflict, and generally both. The people are almost always the actors in the drama, so think about starting with them if possible.

Occasionally the Who might be a fire, a tornado, flash floods or an earthquake. In these fairly rare examples, the freak of nature itself might become the 'actor' in the drama.

If the drama involves two or more people or groups, you need to think which one your readers are more interested in. If an individual trade unionist takes on a big company over some staffing matter and wins, the *Financial Times* would probably start with the company as the first Who:

> Bloggs Incorporated was forced to back down yesterday …

But a trade union paper, and probably the local paper as well, might start with the individual:

> A Manchester sheet metal worker won his case against …

If one of the characters in a story is well known to your readers, then there is no doubt that that person will become the Who of the story. Indeed, in the case of celeb stories, it is the person's name that makes the story. But if the person is not known to your readers, don't use the name in the first paragraph. Work out what it is about him or her which is interesting, what it is that defines the person from the point of view of the story.

A national newspaper might run:

A British couple escaped injury when their hire car fell over a cliff in Spain ...

In this case, the paper is writing about the couple because they are British. Their own local paper will say:

A Cheltenham couple escaped injury ...

The local paper is writing about them because they live in the town.

In the following story, the important thing about the man is not that he sold his firm for £3 million, but that he had built it up without any formal training or tertiary education:

A man who left school without GCSEs yesterday sold his computer firm for £3 million ...

If when you have written the intro, you find that the first idea in it is not a person or group of people, have another look at it and see whether it can be rearranged. So don't write:

New figures released today show that there has been a rise in gun crime ...

But:

More people are being arrested carrying guns ...

WHAT?

This nearly always means: What Happened? Or Did What? Work out the most dramatic thing about the story and make sure you get to it very early on in your first sentence. So the answer to What will almost always involve a verb. Ideally it should be an active verb and should give us a picture of the drama that you are telling us about. Make sure someone (or occasionally an 'actor' such as a tornado) is doing something.

Never use the words 'happened' or 'took place', and try very hard to avoid using the verb 'to be'. Often these verbs make your story very static, and you end up describing a state of affairs rather than someone doing something. So not:

An explosion took place at a paint shop ...

And not:

There has been an explosion at a paint shop ...

But:

An explosion ripped through a paint shop ...

Nearly always your story will involve a person or a group: again, make sure your Who group is doing something active. So not:

A British couple were unhurt when their car ...

But:

A British couple escaped unhurt when ...

With the same active idea in mind, don't start with a negative. So not:

Bromsgrove Council last night decided not to build some new homes ...

But:

Bromsgrove Council last night abandoned plans to build some new homes ...

Very often, especially when covering politics and business, the thing that happened is simply that someone said something. But avoid:

Tony Blair said ...

Go for:

Tony Blair announced/welcomed/revealed/defied critics/negotiated/defended himself/took on his critics ...

All of these give a bit more drama and action to your story. Of course, it is possible to overdo this, and a story which is full of 'hit out', 'attacked', 'defended' and so on can become very chewy and indigestible. But for the first sentence, remember that you have got to persuade your readers to invest some time in the rest of the story, so you need some words that grab their attention.

WHEN?

Newspapers, especially daily or evening ones, almost always give the answer to this question in the first sentence. Evening papers especially like to include the word 'today' in nearly every story, because it gives an up-to-the-minute feeling. Morning papers similarly almost always include 'yesterday' in the first sentence if they possibly can.

Local weekly papers and weekly or monthly magazines are a bit more cautious. Sometimes they skate round it with the use of a present perfect tense:

> A Cheltenham couple have escaped injury ...

Sometimes local papers will simply ignore the time element to obscure the fact that the event happened more than a week before their publication date. Sometimes they back into the story by describing the state of affairs now, rather than the thing that happened. This is discussed in more detail later in this chapter.

WHERE?

Think about this one. A classic agency story will always say very high up, and probably in the intro, where something happened. Obviously it is not necessary with big political stories: if the prime minister says something, we can take it as read that he probably did so somewhere near Downing Street. Similarly with business and financial stories, the Where is not necessary. Of course, if Tony Blair interrupted a holiday in Barbados to pronounce on something, then the story would say so.

Lots of the human interest and quirky stories in the tabloid papers leave the answer to the Where question well down the story. So an odd little story about a poodle surviving in a washing machine often will not mention until nearly the end that it happened in Arizona. Presumably the tabloid editors feel that if they reveal to their readers that the event happened a long way away, some of them will lose interest. This is creeping into the compacts as well now.

WHY?

You might not always need the answer to this in the first sentence. But it is something you should consider. The point about this question is that it gives context to your story. This is not so important in a dramatic story about an earthquake, but can be very important in political, economic or business stories.

There might be a couple of different kinds of Why in a story. It might be that you need to tell your readers why something happened:

Thousands of packets of cholesterol-lowering pills were recalled yesterday after the discovery of a fake version of the drug.

It might be that you need to explain as soon as possible what the significance of something is (the answer to the question: Why are you telling me this?):

The Provisional IRA is to destroy its weapons within two months, after announcing yesterday that it has ended its 35-year campaign of violence.

Here is an example from the B2B magazine *Marketing*:

Jaffa is investing in its first TV ad campaign for 25 years as part of a brand relaunch designed to capitalise on growing consumer concerns about obesity.

This is clear, concise, 27 words, and answering the question Why (new campaign linked to current concerns about obesity) gives it context and depth.

IDEAL LENGTH

The most common type of intro, and the one that is easiest to read, is a single sentence, with at the most one subordinate clause or phrase.

If you gather your information, and construct such a sentence, taking care to answer the question What happened?, you are likely to end up with a sentence of between 20 and 30 words. Intros in tabloid newspapers are usually at the shorter end of this range, perhaps about 18–20 words, and those in more reflective papers such as the *Guardian* are often a bit longer.

A sentence of about 20–25 words can be read out loud easily in one breath. This is a good test. If you can read your intro in one breath, your reader can probably absorb it very easily in one reading. Most news editors would say that an intro which has to be read twice is a failure. So if your intro is more than say 28 words, try to work out which bits you can shorten or throw away. Can you say 'the government' instead of 'the Department of the Environment'? Will Birmingham do at first reference, rather than a suburb of Birmingham? Can you shorten the verb eg. use 'criticized' rather than 'has criticized'? Can you convert an abstract noun to a verb? This is a good idea generally, because it will make the story more active. But it is also likely to save a couple of words. So not:

Residents are furious over the council's decision to go ahead with the expulsion of their association from ...

But:

> Residents are furious because the council decided to expel …

So try to get your sentence down to between 20 and 25 words.

On the other hand, if you have fewer than about 18 words you might not have told your readers enough to make them want to read on:

> A person was slightly hurt in a car crash in Newcastle yesterday.

This is just not interesting enough. It lacks detail, and the more detail you can squeeze in, without making the sentence too hard to follow, the better.

> A young mother had a lucky escape when a lorry jack-knifed in front of her car …

is a much more arresting story.

If you make the intro too short, you run the risk of what some journalists call the 'so what factor'. If you can imagine your readers saying 'So what?' at any point in a story, the story is a failure. And this is particularly the case with the intro. You must convey enough in the intro to convince your readers that the story is worth reading.

THE THREE THINGS TEST

Another good way to check whether your intro is sharp enough, and easy enough to grasp, is to check how many different ideas you have in it. In general a good intro will have at the most three main ideas. If you have four or more, it might be too complicated for your readers to grasp in one quick read.

Here is a good example from *Retail Week*, the B2B magazine for the retail industry:

> Tesco plans to enter the £12.5 billion furniture market in the New Year, in a pitch that could hurt specialists such as MFI.

This is an excellent intro – 23 words, straight and to the point. It starts with a big Who, one of the biggest players in the area covered by this magazine. There is interesting detail such as the figure, and the second verb, 'hurt', is active and arresting.

Count the ideas: Tesco, the furniture market, and the possible effect on MFI. I don't count the time element as a separate idea. It is essential there and is easily grasped. The story went on to say that 'big ticket furniture items' such as dining tables and chairs would be offered on the Tesco website.

Consider what would have happened if the reporter had tried to squeeze that point into the intro as well:

> Tesco plans to enter the £12.5 billion furniture market in the New Year, offering big ticket items such as dining tables and chairs on its website, in a pitch that could hurt specialists such as MFI.

There are three ways to check whether this would be the best possible intro:

- The word count: it is 36 words, just too long to be easily grasped in one glance.
- It can barely be read in one breath, certainly only by taking a very deep breath and expending every bit of air.
- There are two, or possibly one and a half, more ideas in it. As well as the three in the original, there is detail about the furniture and the point about the website. That is just too many ideas for the reader to get hold of easily.

Here is a great example of an intro by a reporter who had not heard about the Three Things Test:

> An ear, nose and throat specialist today said that with hindsight he should not have examined the groin and breasts of a Swedish woman referred to him because she was having dizzy spells.

It is hard to work out where to begin with this. It is undeniably a good story. Medical stories are often interesting. This appears to be some kind of hearing, so there is conflict there and that always makes for a good news story. The physical detail is of course interesting. So what is wrong? At 33 words, it is slightly over length, but even that might be okay. The problem is that it is indigestible. There is simply too much stuff here for the reader to absorb it easily at one glance. There are at least six different ideas:

1 the specialist and his specialism
2 the point about hindsight
3 the medical examination
4 the areas of the patient's body that he examined
5 the fact that she was a Swedish woman
6 the referral and the dizzy spells

That is at least a couple of ideas too many for a reader to get hold of in one quick reading.

> An ear, nose and throat specialist admitted today that he should not have examined the groin and breasts of a patient whom he was treating for dizzy spells.

This is 28 words. If he had been a cardiologist or a brain surgeon, we could have saved another couple of words. It is essential to keep the doctor's specialism in, as this highlights the strangeness of his examination. There is a tension, an unexpectedness, between his specialism and the examination, which is essential to make sure the intro persuades the reader to continue reading. The hindsight point is not really necessary, and neither is the point about her being Swedish. We know she is female, because she has breasts, and I feel that 'patient' is a much better word than 'woman', since it adds to the tension by emphasizing the doctor/patient relationship. This version follows the Three Things Test, gets to the drama quickly, and is easy to grasp in one swift read.

GET PLENTY OF DETAIL

An intro along the lines of 'man injured in car crash' is simply not interesting because it is short on detail. The more you can tell us about the man, the crash, the lucky escape and so on, the better the story will be. Have a look at this example:

> Handfuls of lentils and baked beans were pelted at eviction officers yesterday as they tried to move anti-road protesters from tree-top camps in Dalkeith Country Park.

This is 26 words, a good length, and it is very dramatic. It is very slightly indigestible, and I don't mean because of the beans, but simply because of the variety of ideas we have here. If we discount the Where, and treat the road protesters and their tree-top camps as one idea, it passes the Three Things Test. What it certainly does not lack is detail. The picture we get of the protesters, the eviction officers, the tree tops and especially the lentils and beans, brings the whole thing to life. Substituting 'food' would ruin it. It would be slightly easier to read, but would have lost the essential colour.

It is difficult to get just enough colour and detail to make the story interesting, but not so much as to make it too hard to grasp in one quick read. It is worth looking at intros on the same lively story in several papers, and seeing exactly how the reporter manages this balancing act.

HOTSPOT AT THE VERY BEGINNING

As we have said, good news intros should be around 25 words long, but the first half must be arresting and attention-grabbing. One example I use for my students is this: Imagine you are rushing into a pub with a great story to tell. All your friends are standing there with their lagers, and they are already having an interesting conversation about something. You have got to say something dramatic quickly because their attention is already engaged elsewhere. You have in effect got a couple of seconds, perhaps the first 12 words of a potential story. So don't start with:

> The air quality sub-group of the Environment Committee of Islington Borough Council has last night decided …

Instead go for:

> Air pollution in Islington could be cut by a third if new plans …

Make sure you have an arresting idea, and if possible an arresting word or phrase, in the first half of the intro. The more frequently a word appears in common use, the less meaning it carries. Make sure you have some words in the first half of your intro which carry enough meaning to make your readers sit up and pay attention. I call them '**listen-to-me**' words.

> A tornado ripped the roofs off houses in …

is so much more arresting than

> A strong wind blew the roofs off …

Make sure you also have plenty of action. Make sure the verbs tell us about people doing things, not what things are like.

Paul Nicholas from the *News of the World* spoke to our students once about writing news, and discussed the well-documented point that news stories carry more verbs than other kinds of writing. A verb involves someone doing something, or something happening. He pointed out that in a news story, nothing happens until the next verb. It is essential to keep the verbs coming, to keep the story active.

In the process of refining your intro, spend a minute confirming in your head what the story really is, what it is that has happened. Make sure your first verb relates exactly to that point. If it doesn't, it probably means you have started with some explanatory or interpretative point, which would be better at the end of the intro, or perhaps in the second paragraph.

At the same time, check that the intro answers the question 'What happened?' Inexperienced reporters sometimes find they have answered the question 'What is it like now?' This is what experienced hacks call 'backing into the story'. You sometimes see this type of construction in local papers:

> A Wellingborough mother of three is recovering in hospital after she lost her footing, fell into the Nene and was carried over a weir …

Sometimes this formula is used to try to bring the story up to date, because the actual news event happened a while ago. I am not sure this is a good idea. Realistically most of the readers will not have heard about it, so I can't see anything wrong in starting with the drama of the news point:

> Three children watched in horror as their mother fell into the Nene and was carried over …

Or:

> A Wellingborough mother escaped serious injury when she fell into the Nene and was carried …

Some local paper reporters are also very fond of the opening:

> Police are searching ...

Or even worse:

> Police are hunting ...

This is a classic answer to 'What is it like now?' rather than 'What happened?' Of course, police are searching for someone. It's what they are paid to do. You could start 20 stories in a local paper every week like that. But there are ways round this. Look at this example from the *Birmingham Mail*:

> A sex attacker who terrorised a mum as she pushed her baby's buggy through a Midland churchyard was being hunted by police today.

This story appeared two days after the event, and reporters on evening papers particularly hate to have anything other than 'today' as the answer to the question When? But by starting with the crime, with plenty of listen-to-me words, and giving the reader a good picture of the event, it is possible to get the today point in and avoid the tired old 'Police are hunting …'

This intro is also a good example of one of the fairly rare times when the Where is well worth including in the intro. It adds a real frisson: whether readers think of churchyards as peaceful or as spooky, either way it makes a dramatic picture in their minds.

For another way to help young journalists see what the news point of a story is, I am indebted to Oliver Wates, a former colleague from Reuters, and now a full-time trainer. Imagine you have discovered a very interesting piece of news. It is quite complicated, and it is essential that you tell a particular friend about it. But that friend is leaving town any minute by train.

You rush to the station. The train is ready to depart. You get onto the platform and find the friend just settling into a seat. You run alongside the carriage just as the train begins to move. You might manage one brief, and easily understood sentence, before that train pulls out. It is not going to be:

> In a move which will astonish Conservative voters up and down the country, following the leadership ballot this week, Mrs Thatcher ...

But:

> Mrs Thatcher resigned today ...

The first example starts with the interpretation and the background. The second tells us what happened.

Quite often it is easy to see what the action is, and get it into the first paragraph. Bombs go off, arrests are made, government policies are changed, and it is not difficult to see what the next bit of news is. But inexperienced writers, confronted with a long and complicated series of events, perhaps after a court case, often find it hard to see the wood for the trees. Here is a three-step formula I use in such cases:

1 Imagine you are making a short film of the events you have heard about in your morning's reporting. Make the film in your head, from the beginning. For example, landlord wakes up, hears a noise downstairs in his pub, goes down, opens door to bar, finds two intruders, challenges them, etc.
2 'Watch' the film through in your head, and try to pinpoint the most dramatic moment, the tiny clip which would be the trailer. Freeze-frame on this scene. Perhaps it is the moment when the landlord picks up a chair and hits one of the intruders over the head. This might be a few seconds of the trailer for the film. It is also the intro to the news story.
3 Picture that frame of the film, write your intro, and then make sure your readers can see the same event when they read your intro:

> A pub landlord confronted two hooded burglars and knocked one to the floor with a chair last night ...

This 'making the film' approach reveals several points about a good intro. It helps you to focus on the most dramatic point of the story, and it helps with another essential – in a good dramatic news story, the reporter must give the readers a *picture*. If there has been a piece of genuine drama, make sure you can see it in your mind's eye. Then tell your readers about it in such a way that they can see it too.

INTROS FOR LESS DRAMATIC STORIES

The most newsworthy thing, which makes the best news story, is something that has not happened before. It is a bit like those non-verbal reasoning tests, where there are five triangles with blobs inside them, they all look very similar and you have to pick out the one that is slightly different. A good reporter does that with a news story.

There might, for example, be three stories about golden weddings in a local area in one week. A good reporter will find something different about each couple so that each story is different. In one case there was a surprise visit from a son who lives in Australia. In another the wife had proposed to the husband. In another they had conducted a long-distance courtship. The good reporter finds what is different about three potentially very similar situations.

A court reporter might hear three similar shoplifting cases. Again the good reporter will spot something different about each one. Perhaps in one case there was a police chase down the high street; in another some expensive sexy lingerie was stolen; in another maybe there was an impassioned plea from a lawyer that the accused had three children to look after and should not be sent to jail.

Plenty of good news stories are not about dramatic events, they are about reports, campaigns, government or council plans or decisions. This is when you have to relate your story carefully to the news values discussed in Chapter 1. What is the point that will most interest your readers? Is it that the story is relevant to them?:

> Islington residents face big council tax rises …
> Smoking will be banned …
> A million children in Britain are obese …

If it is not really relevant to your readers, you have got to think why else they might be interested. Is it because it is a quirky human interest story? Is it funny? Is it ironic? If there is no innate drama in your story, you need to make sure there is some other kind of tension in your intro. Irony is sometimes the way to do this.

Here is an example from the *Press Gazette*, the B2B magazine for journalists:

> News agency Splash made a mockery of Tony Blair's 'secret' holiday security arrangements by locating him before his plane had even touched down.

This intro had got a lot going for it – indeed, it made the lead story in the magazine. The readers are journalists, therefore they are interested in one of their own scoring a success like this. The agency is known to many of the readers. The story of the prime minister's holidays has been a long-running and interesting one. There are listen-to-me words, including 'mockery' and 'secret', which give an edge to the sentence. The intro gives us a good dramatic 'picture' – the point that they were ahead with the story before he arrived. And it is all the ideal length – 23 words – easy to read in one breath and absorb entirely at one quick read.

There was a lot more to the story, quotes from Downing Street, quotes from the agency about how it got and followed the story. But the essence of it is summed up in that first paragraph.

INTRO CHECKLIST

1   Always count the words: aim for between 20 and 25, preferably in one flowing sentence.
2   Make sure it tells us the *most important* thing in the story.
3   If you had *only* these 25 words for the whole story – make sure your reader has been told something interesting.
4   Don't start with a subsidiary clause: go for the action point first, in case the train leaves before you can finish the sentence.
5   Count the number of main ideas and aim for three, or two if the story is very dramatic. Four or more different ideas make the intro indigestible.
6   The first 10 words are the most important – make sure they grab your reader.
7   Mention a person by name *only* if your average reader knows who s/he is.
8   Don't emphasize the negative: tell us something that did happen, not something that didn't.
9   Don't begin with time or place: the Who and the What Happened are far more important than the Where and When.
10 Don't begin a news story with a direct quote. You rarely see this in news stories, although it can work for a feature. If the actual news point is something someone said, it will be far easier to grasp in reported speech.
11 Use active rather than passive verbs: not 'A shop was burgled last night …' but 'Burglars smashed into a shop …'
12 Remember listen-to-me words: 'not' Bloxwich Council is reviewing its policy on providing affordable housing for asylum seekers following …' but 'Homeless asylum seekers will get priority …'('homeless' and 'asylum seekers' are both more attention-grabbing phrases than 'Bloxwich Council' and 'reviewing').

SCENARIOS FOR DISCUSSION

SCENARIO 1: SCHOOL TRIP DRAMA

A party of girls from St James's School, Cleeve, were on a mountain challenge exercise which ended this morning. They had to walk over a route in the Black Mountains in Wales, in groups of four, and were met at checkpoints by leaders. When one group failed to pass a checkpoint after four hours, rescue parties set out and an RAF helicopter was called in to help with the search.

Rescuers searched for two hours before discovering that the girls had made their way straight back to the base camp by taxi after one of them sprained her ankle. They had called the taxi on a mobile phone which one of them had with her. The RAF is considering sending a bill to the school for the helicopter.

This is quite a complicated chain of events, and the reporter needs to absorb the information and sit well back from it to try to work out what to tell the reader first. The tension between the drama of the helicopter and the fact that the girls got a taxi back should be in the intro. It is that picture, of the helicopter searching and the girls in the taxi, which you need to give your readers first. Try to make sure you tell us first about the thing that happens least often. People get lost and found on mountains pretty often. Helicopters search pretty often. But it is extremely rare that a helicopter searches for people who are actually safe at home. This then must be the point of the intro. Here are two possible versions:

The RAF scrambled a helicopter today to search for schoolgirls feared lost in the Welsh mountains, only to discover that they had returned to base by taxi.

This at 27 words is quite long, but it may be impossible to get it into less. Notice the listen-to-me words: scrambled, helicopter, search, feared, lost. Note that the reader can easily grasp the tension between the helicopter and the taxi. Note that we have got the Where and When as well.

Here is another possibility:

A school may be billed by the RAF after a helicopter searched for four girls feared missing in the Welsh Mountains but who had returned to base in a taxi.

This version gets in the interesting point about the possible bill for the school, which emphasizes the futility of the search. My reservation about this one is that it is in danger of failing the Three Things Test: the bill point may just be one idea too many, and it is hypothetical rather than a fact.

SCENARIO 2: PROSTATE CANCER TRIAL RESULTS

Approximately 21,000 men are diagnosed with prostate cancer every year in the UK – and over 10,000 men die from prostate cancer annually in the UK. It is the biggest single cancer affecting men.

Prostate cancer is known to 'feed' on the men's hormone testosterone.

Treatment for the cancer can involve surgical removal of the prostate, and/or radio-therapy. There are also hormone treatments but these can cause impotence.

A big trial has been conducted in 23 countries, involving 8,000 men. It tested the effects of prescribing a drug called Casodex, which 'starves' the cancer by preventing testosterone getting to it.

The drug stopped the disease from spreading in 42 per cent of the men in the trial.

Casodex allows the testosterone to stay in the bloodstream, but prevents it from reaching the prostate.

There are several possible approaches to this. Decide who you want to make the Who of the story. Is it cancer sufferers, the drug itself, scientists or the trial? This will depend on the newspaper or magazine you are writing for. For a national newspaper, the Who might be cancer sufferers. But that may be a bit too obvious. Nationals, especially those that cover health issues thoroughly, could run a story on the lines of new hope for cancer sufferers every day of the week. So although the relevance-to-the-reader point suggests overwhelmingly that the Who should be cancer patients, plenty of newspapers might want to start with scientists just for the sake of variety. For a journal for doctors, the Who might well be scientists, or the trial itself. For a regional paper in the area where the research was conducted, it might well be

Scientists at Birmingham University have had a breakthrough ...

Here are some possibilities:

Scientists have developed a new drug for prostate cancer which prevents the spread of the disease without causing impotence.

This is short (19 words) and easy to grasp. It is perhaps quite dry, and rather lacking in people, but it does tell us the point about not causing impotence, which must be one of the newest and most important points in the story.

Prostate cancer sufferers may benefit from a new drug which has been shown to halt the spread of the disease without causing impotence.

This gets the human angle and the relevance-to-the-reader point in very early on, and also includes the point about impotence. This version is fine, easy to grasp, and has got the main point. It may be a bit short on listen-to-me words.

> A massive international trial has shown that a new drug curbs prostate cancer without causing impotence.

This again is brief, (16 words), but with enough points to make us want to read on. Unlike the two above, this version has some rather more dramatic listen-to-me words such as 'massive', 'international' and 'curbs'. The word 'massive' may be a bit overused in news writing; it pops up perhaps a bit too often in an attempt to jazz-up all sorts of stories about parking fines or new buildings.

SCENARIO 3: BA IN RACIAL DISCRIMINATION CLAIM

> After an air crash in Manchester in 1985 when 54 people died, air hostesses and stewards on British Airways planes have been supplied with smoke hoods.
> These hoods go over the person's entire head and are sealed around the neck. They protect from toxic fumes, to enable cabin crew to fight onboard fires. For this reason, BA stewards cannot have beards.
> Two Sikhs were turned down as stewards because of this – they were told they would have to be willing to remove their turbans and trim their beards.
> They began a claim of racial discrimination. This claim was withdrawn today when BA agreed to try to develop new smoke hoods.
> The men were Naryan Singh and Vinder Sandhu.

This is another complicated scenario, and the reporter needs to work out carefully what exactly has happened, and then work out which is the most important group to make the Who of the story: which group will be most important to the reader. There are other pitfalls with this story too. The men cannot be said to have won a case, since the case was withdrawn.

A local paper based where the two men live, would clearly make them the first Who:

> Two Ealing men dropped a race discrimination claim …

On the other hand, a business publication, especially one for the aircraft industry, would make the airline the Who:

> British Airways has agreed to try to develop new smoke hoods …

Here are some possibilities:

> Two Sikhs dropped a race discrimination case against British Airways today after the airline agreed to try to develop fire-fighting hoods which can accommodate turbans and beards.

This intro homes in on what actually happened today, which is that the case was dropped, and gives enough of the facts to enable the reader to understand what happened and why. There are some listen-to-me words, including 'race discrimination' and 'British Airways'. It is such a well-known company that its doings are bound to be interesting. There is no point in using the phrase 'smoke hood' in the first paragraph, because it would not be understood without explanation, whereas 'fire-fighting equipment', though more general, can be understood on its own.

> British Airways today agreed to try to develop fire-fighting hoods to accommodate turbans after a race discrimination claim by two Sikhs who were turned down as air stewards.

This is the version for a business publication whose readers are sure to consider British Airways an interesting start to the story. The intro is quite wordy, but that may be inevitable because it is a complicated story. British Airways itself is interesting. There is plenty of tension, with the mentions of 'race discrimination', 'claim', and 'turned down'.

STRUCTURE PART 1:
THE INVERTED PYRAMID

There are two main ways of telling a story. One is the chronological approach, starting at or before the beginning of a series of events, and working through to the end. The other is to start *'in medias res'* – in the middle of things. This phrase comes from the Latin poet Horace, who advised young poets that when writing an epic they should begin in the middle of things, at a dramatic moment. He might have been, indeed to a certain extent he was, teaching news writing, since epic poetry is about big newsworthy events.

In the 1970s, the *Sunday Times* serialized Jan Morris's book *Conundrum*, about her sex change. The book begins with the writer's early life, from the first realization that he was really a woman in a man's body, the hormone treatment, and then the trip to Casablanca for the operation (which could not be carried out legally in Britain at that time).

But where did the newspaper serialization begin? Not in that way, but with a picture of the writer sitting in a café in Casablanca, thinking about going under the knife the next day. There is no doubt that the most dramatic point about this story is the actual operation. Morris can't describe that in detail, because he was under an anaesthetic. The next best thing is to describe his feelings just before it. Almost the whole of the first of the three extracts was taken up with the operation and the time just before and after it.

This was effectively a news feature, but the principle is the same, that in newspaper writing it is almost always best to grab your readers' attention in the very first paragraph, and not expect them to wade through a lot of material before getting to the drama. This approach is often described in terms of an inverted pyramid (or triangle), which I have set out in Figure 4.1.

The idea is that a story starts with the most dramatic, most important point, the second most dramatic point comes next, the third next, and so on.

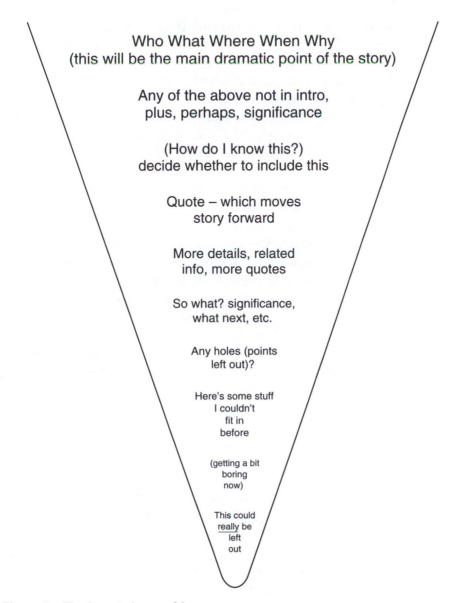

Who What Where When Why
(this will be the main dramatic point of the story)

Any of the above not in intro,
plus, perhaps, significance

(How do I know this?)
decide whether to include this

Quote – which moves
story forward

More details, related
info, more quotes

So what? significance,
what next, etc.

Any holes (points
left out)?

Here's some stuff
I couldn't
fit in
before

(getting a bit
boring
now)

This could
really be
left
out

Figure 2   The inverted pyramid

This is set out using a pyramid (or some people call it a triangle) drawn upside down, with the widest, heaviest part at the top.

It is interesting that pyramids when they are the usual way up are very stable structures, which is one of the reasons they have survived for so long. A pyramid the other way up is the very opposite of a stable structure. It is unstable and highly likely to crash over. That idea of an inbuilt tension, something slightly unnerving, is exactly what a good news story has.

Many news stories are not read to the end. If the story has been written in the inverted pyramid style, and readers move on to something after the first few paragraphs, they have still been told the most important points.

Another reason for following the inverted pyramid principle is to do with the way newspapers and magazines used to be produced. Each story was made up of lines of metal type (produced by a Linotype machine). These were then fitted into heavy metal frames, split into columns by rules. Sub-editors, when they were editing stories for print, were very good at estimating how long a story needed to be to fit the space allocated to it on a page. But things did not always work out quite right, and at the last moment before going to press, stories were often cut from the bottom to make them fit the page, or to allow room for a new, late-breaking story. It was essential therefore that the information in the story became less and less important towards the bottom.

News agencies almost always use the inverted pyramid principle, so that if the subscriber is just going to press or on air, and does not have time to read and analyse the whole story, the most important point of the story can be included because it is in the first paragraph.

Within the confines of the inverted pyramid, it is usual to try to get an arresting quote into the third or fourth paragraph. This idea is generally followed because quotes make the story as lively as possible and keep people in the forefront. The best stories usually have a quote here which moves the story forward and tells us the next most important thing. Very often the quote will actually form part of the news point, perhaps it explains the significance of the event, perhaps it tells us what might happen next.

I have set out below (Scenario 1) a news story about a freak tornado which hit Birmingham in the summer of 2005. I have constructed it from several different stories in newspapers and on the web. It has the main point at the beginning, with each point gradually decreasing in importance further down the story.

Another feature of this story is what some journalists call the 'washing-line' construction. There is a middle section of eyewitness accounts which is itself carefully constructed. Some of these could be taken out entirely (in the way that different items could be removed from a washing line when they are dry). This would not cause any problems with the story, which would still fit into the inverted pyramid structure.

Notice, however, that this central section is an inverted pyramid itself, with the best and most dramatic eyewitness material at the top, and less dramatic quotes further down. You often see this washing-line arrangement in the reporting of a big dramatic event, where reporters assemble as much eyewitness material as they can, so that the page editors have the freedom to use as much as they need for whatever spread they are planning.

Another way to use this section would be to put all the quotes in a sidebar or box elsewhere on the page. This point is discussed in Chapter 13. You also see the washing-line arrangement with something like a big takeover or other City event, where reporters will contact various analysts and other commentators. Then, so long as enough are used to keep the balance, the subs have the freedom if necessary to cut some of them to fit the page.

SCENARIO 1: TORNADO HITS BIRMINGHAM

A tornado struck Birmingham yesterday, ripping roofs off houses, hurling cars across roads and injuring at least 12 people.

Intro: 19 words, quite short, but story is so dramatic that this is fine. Who: tornado; What: struck; Where: Birmingham; When: yesterday. Rest of para gives drama/people. Everything for an understanding of the story, and a picture of the drama is here.

Trees were uprooted and shopfronts blown in as the twister tore through the southern part of the city.

Para 2: This is an elaboration of the intro – giving more drama and picture, and pinning down the Where. This is important, Birmingham is well known to many people.

Three people were seriously injured by what one shopkeeper described as 'bricks, slates and other debris whizzing down the road'.

Para 3: Vital here to sort out the injuries to people as soon as possible. Also, a good quote here, which takes story forward, explaining how the injuries occurred, and gives us another dramatic picture.

The freak weather tore a 300-yard zigzag through King's Heath and Sparkbrook, leaving a trail of damage and so many injuries that paramedics set up an emergency triage centre at the scene.

Para 4: More dramatic detail – giving us exact information about Where, more about what exactly happened – and the interesting new information about the triage centre at the scene. This gives us two more graphic pictures of the events.

The tornado, which lasted about 10 minutes, turned the sky a dull brown, blew part of the roof off a primary school, and littered the area with glass, bricks, furniture. Everything from shoes to fruit was torn

Para 5: Again, more pictures, more detail, and the interesting and dramatic point, backed up lower down, about children being lifted off their feet. This paragraph also pins down exactly how long the tornado lasted. Notice throughout the story the use of listen-to-me words:

from shop displays. For a few minutes the air was filled with flying debris and children spoke of being lifted off their feet.

tornado, twister, freak, ripping, hurling, torn.

Witnesses said the sudden onslaught at 2.30 pm after torrential rain had been short-lived but terrifying, with initial attempts to run for cover blocked by falling trees or a hail of debris.

Para 6: More detail about time, more picture, and more drama about people.

Brian Cassidy, 30, a carpenter from Balsall Heath, said the wind virtually 'unscrewed' a roof from a house, lifting it with a twisting motion. 'I could see grown men on a garage forecourt crying, holding their ears. It was like breaking matches.'

Para 7: The story now moves into the washing-line mode. There were probably any number of interviews available with people who had experienced the events. Generally a reporter would be expected, with an event like this, to obtain as much eyewitness material as possible. This middle section could include as many of them as the paper has room for. However, there is no doubt that a reporter would be expected to put all the best ones at the top of this section, with the quotes becoming less dramatic or newsworthy further down.

Diana Taylor was at home with her 16-year-old daughter and a 14-year-old niece in Small Heath when the tornado ripped her roof off.

Notice the variety in these quotes, with different experiences from the various people. One is an eyewitness who saw a roof being blown away. Another was cowering in her home. One was a child, another saw a dramatic moment involving a baby.

'Everything went black and I opened the front door to take a look,' she said. 'I really had to push the door hard to close it, the wind was so powerful. I was in the living room and the floor rose up. We were all screaming. We ran to the bottom of the stairs, and were hiding there when we heard the living room roof crash in. I'm not sure I've got much of a house left.'

Ciaran Daly, 10, was riding a scooter in Saltley when the wind struck. 'We were coming from our house when we saw trees and bushes shaking, and big black clouds. The wind got so strong it blew me into the air.' Kamran Ishtiaq, 22, who owns a supermarket in King's Heath, watched in horror as a woman just managed to free her baby from a buggy which was then tossed across the road.

King's Heath High Street was sealed off after a car park attendant's wooden hut was blown from one side to the other, splintering the front of an Iceland store.

Para 11: Story moves to a wider context, with some 'official' interventions – police sealing off a road.

A spokesman for West Midlands Ambulance Service said that it had treated 19 casualties. Three were seriously hurt with broken limbs. None have life-threatening injuries but last night medical teams, police and firefighters were still searching damaged buildings for other possible victims.

Para 12: Then we move to tying up loose ends. Details of numbers of casualties, filling in blanks about actual injuries mentioned earlier, details about the ongoing rescue operation.

Staff at Heartlands and Selly Oak hospitals treated a number of casualties for minor injuries.

Firefighters said 15 tenders had tried to cope initially with the chaos in the square half-mile round Ladypool Road.

David Elliott, of the Meteorological Office's Birmingham weather centre, said the city had been in the path of a line of very heavy thunderstorms as they crossed the country. 'It is very warm, moist, humid, sticky air, perfect conditions for mini-tornadoes.'

Para 15: Having finished the human drama part of the story, and cleared up any detail about casualties, the story moves to the wider picture of how it happened, with analysis from weather experts.

The stricken area is less than half a mile from the scene of a storm in 1999 when high winds uprooted a roadside tree which fell onto several vehicles, killing three people.

Para 16: And an interesting bit of background about a serious freak storm six years before.

The freak weather conditions also caused a second much smaller tornado that struck Peterborough, damaging roofs and trees. Heavy rain warnings printed in red dominated the Met Office's website throughout the day as downpours moved in belts across the whole country south of the Scottish border.

Conclusion: Tying up a few loose ends here, clearly the Peterborough tornado, though much smaller, is worth including. The story really does begin to fizzle out now, and some papers chose to stitch in general material about the weather here. Others cross-referenced to weather reports on other pages. Some took the opportunity for sidebars, either more detail and analysis on the previous day's freak weather conditions, or on the likelihold of tornadoes in Britain (about 33 a year apparently).

SCENARIO 2: NEW TV FOOD SHOW LAUNCH

Here is a very different story from *Restaurant*, the B2B magazine for the restaurant world.

'F' ME, IT'S GORDON: RAMSAY AND COREN FORM TV DOUBLE ACT AS CHANNEL 4 LAUNCHES NO-HOLDS BARRED RESTAURANT PROGRAMME

A new weekly food show starring Gordon Ramsay and co-presented by *The Times'* restaurant critic Giles Coren will run on Channel 4 for nine weeks from late October until Christmas.

Para 1: Good straight new intro – the names are the listen-to-me words here – Gordon Ramsay is extremely newsworthy. The main facts are all here. If we weren't told anything else, we would have the main point.

Produced by Optomen Television, it's called *The F Word* and, according to the pre-publicity, it's to be set 'in a glamorous restaurant location with an "audience" of specially invited diners'.

Para 2: The second most important point is in the second paragraph: the dramatic title of the show, plus a picture of what it will be like.

A three-course dinner for up to 60 diners, including chefs, food writers and members of the public, will be prepared during the course of each programme, with action coming live from the kitchen, bar, dining room and cellar of the location. The programme also aims to deliver 'up to the minute food news' and 'go undercover to expose bad food, bad service and bad value on behalf of the customer'.

Para 3: More detail of what the show will actually be, gives a fairly complete picture of what will happen. Also a couple of other points about the show.

'It won't be edited, it's all going out live and I'll be running the kitchen for each show,' said Ramsay. 'As well as having a "chef idol" element to it, we'll be kicking off with a campaign to get women back into the kitchen. It's a programme with clear objectives.'

Para 4: The all-important quote from the main character, and a few more details about the programme.

Coren said of the programme: 'If people think Gordon is a rude bastard, wait until they hear me.'

Para 5: Story fizzles out, with a quote from Coren, which is a good quote, and rounds the story off nicely, but is the most expendable point of the story – just as it should be.

BEWARE THE PIZZA EFFECT

The two stories above have a clear news point, and there is no real difficulty working out which material should be high up. Often, however, a reporter has to construct a news story from much more diffuse material. A good example is when reporting a speech. Very often the speaker will mention several points, sometimes quite unrelated, and the reporter has to decide, taking into account the readers and recent events, what the main point is.

We often have newsworthy people coming into the journalism department at City University to speak to the students who then write up a news story. There can sometimes be a tendency for students to cobble together all the bits and pieces they have got from the talk, and put them all into their news story. This is what I call the 'pizza effect': it reminds you of when someone has decided to order lots of different extra toppings: a bit of ham, some tinned pineapple, mushrooms, perhaps a few sun-dried tomatoes. This doesn't make the greatest pizza, and the approach won't make the greatest news story either.

Emily Thornberry, our local MP, came in to talk to the students. Here are some of the points she talked about:

- How and why she had voted against the government over the 90-day detention for terrorism suspects
- The use of ASBOs in Islington
- The problems caused in some areas by drug taking and prostitution
- Her relationship with the press and the press coverage of her children's schooling
- Plans for a new secondary school in Islington
- The problems for women in succeeding in politics
- Labour's record in helping the poor

You can't hope to get all this different material into a news story, and deciding which bits to go for is one of the hardest things for inexperienced reporters. The vote against the government had been covered in detail for several days, and she did not say anything particularly new. Certainly if a reporter went for that angle, it was then very difficult to stitch in some other material about schooling. On the other hand, going for the angle about press coverage of her children's schooling could at least have led on to the other points about the difficulties of women in politics and perhaps the new secondary school.

But for sure, simply sticking all these different points in does not make for a coherent news story. You must decide on an angle and go for it, and then construct a story with points related to that angle. Then you hope that the reporter from a rival paper doesn't choose a totally different angle, and that your news editor prefers that one.

SUGGESTION FOR FURTHER DISCUSSION

Here is another scenario for a news story for a local paper. Work out the most dramatic point, and that will be at the top of the pyramid. Then decide on the next most dramatic thing, the next thing it is essential for the reader to know in order to understand the story. This will be the second paragraph. Underline all the quotes, and then decide which one is the most telling. Make sure it is not only a lively quote, but that it takes the story forward. As you go along, make sure you don't leave any 'holes' – that it, essential bits of information that a new reader would need.

Sit back far enough from the story to see the bigger picture – it is clearly extremely relevant that there has been an attack here before.

SCENARIO 3: ATTACK ON BLUNTFORD SHOP OWNER

You are a reporter in a weekly paper, *The Bluntford Recorder*, in Bluntford, a North London borough, and you have obtained the following information. It would make a story of between 280 and 300 words.

A statement from Bluntford Police said:

> We are urgently seeking information about a violent attack on a shop owner in Parkway early yesterday evening. At about 6.30 in the evening a man entered Sounds Great, a record shop at 342 Parkway Road. The owner, Mr John Naish, had his back to the door. The man hit Mr Naish on the head once, and then again as he tried to call for help. The man then escaped with a heavy cash till containing £175. We have no description of the assailant. We are anxious for anyone who was in that area at the time to contact us on 020 77771212.

A spokesman for the Whitemoor Hospital said:

> 'Mr John Naish was admitted to the hospital yesterday evening with a fractured skull. He has had an operation and is stable.'

Detective Chief Inspector Jayne Dallowey of Parkway CID said:

> 'This was a horrendous and cowardly attack on a shopkeeper just trying to go about his normal everyday business. We are anxious to hear from anyone who may have any information about what happened. The till was large and awkward to carry and some-one must have seen the suspect making off with it. We believe he had someone to help him and it's possible they made off in a vehicle. There were plenty of people around at that time. We urge anyone who saw anything unusual, even if it seems to be unimportant, to contact us.'

Mr Naish's wife Jenni, who owns and runs the record shop with him, said:

> 'John is going to be OK, but he is not well enough yet to talk to the police. All he has been able to say is that a man hit him with something heavy. Yes I opened the shop as usual today. I have to make a living. I am nervous, and we shall have to think about some sort of CCTV. John is 45.'

You check your database for similar attacks in the area. In January last year Jayson Dauntsey, 35, was dragged from his shop, Good Value Grocer, at 338 Parkway Road and beaten to death with iron bars. The attack took place at lunchtime after a dispute the previous evening over a £5 phone card. Two youths, both aged 17, were jailed for seven years in December for manslaughter. After Mr Dauntsey's death, John Naish warned that Parkway Road had become a lawless place where criminals were guaranteed an easy escape. He told the *Recorder* then: 'I've had several problems here and there are never any police around. Things are getting worse and stretches of Parkway Road are very dangerous.'

Mr Dauntsey's brother George, who now runs the Good Value Grocer said today:

> 'I can't believe something like this has happened, after what happened to my brother. I don't feel this is a safe place. Every day we hear of bad things that have happened. We need the police to clean up these people, they know the ones who are causing all the problems. I was here last night when Mr Naish was attacked. It took the police maybe 10 to 15 minutes to get here.'

Ayse Kemal runs the Kemal café which is between the Good Value Grocer and Sounds Great. She said today:

> 'We are stuck in the middle of these terrible things and I don't feel safe. Anything could happen any time.'

STRUCTURE PART 2: THE NEWS STORY AS ANSWERS

Another way of looking at how to structure a news story, which can be seen in parallel to the inverted pyramid principle, is by considering it as a set of answers.

The news story should be one half of a dialogue with the reader. You begin by telling her the most interesting piece of information you have. Imagine her taking that in, and then asking: 'Good heavens, so why was that?' Or: 'How dreadful, were many people hurt?' Or: 'Does this mean the prime minister will have to resign?' Or maybe, if the story seemed very far-fetched: 'Are you sure?'

The best news story will be one where the second paragraph answers whichever question the majority of readers of that publication would have in their minds when they have read the first. The third paragraph will answer the questions the majority of readers would have in their minds when they have heard the second, and so on. So the secret when writing the story is to try to put yourself in the position of the average reader. You need to imagine that person, sitting beside you or leaning over your shoulder. Put yourself in that person's shoes, and distance yourself from the story so you can see it from the new reader's point of view. This is one of the hardest things for inexperienced reporters to do. It shows why it is so important to know who your readers are. Whatever publication you are writing for, from the *Financial Times* to the *Sun*, you need always to think about your readers, work out what they want to know about an event, and describe it in the same sequence as if you were having a conversation.

Reporters on a local or regional paper need to be clear about the viewpoints and concerns of readers in their area. Reporters on specialist magazines need to know what sort of people are reading their publication, and what their concerns are. Of course, reporters at big international agencies have a different challenge because they are aiming at different groups of readers/subscribers all over the world. This is one of the main reasons why they must remain impartial. The *Daily Mail* can take a strong line on some political issues, because it believes that's what its readers want to hear, but the agency reporter is aiming at the *Guardian* as well, so she needs to steer a straight course, presenting the facts without comment or undue emphasis.

Agencies have to make their stories very clear, with all the essential information in the right place so their reporters become very adept at weaving in short phrases which give essential background as the story progresses. The downside of this is that there is a danger that these phrases turn into clichés: 'oil-rich Dubai' or 'war-torn Iraq'.

It is very easy for a beginner to miss out some vital point early on in a news story. This is known in journalism as a **hole**. Following a question-and-answer technique, and being careful to imagine the average reader sitting beside you asking questions, is one way of avoiding this problem.

The first 'average reader' of a story is of course the sub-editor who is assigned the story to read through and edit. There is a more detailed discussion of sub-editing in Chapter 12. But the very first sub, the first average person to read a story, should be the reporter. It is essential to develop what I call the 'sub's eye': the ability to distance yourself from the story enough to imagine that you are the first reader, the person who doesn't actually know what happened or why. It takes a while to develop this skill, a sort of mental switching off and pretending in your mind that you are the reader. One technique that might help is to save the story on the computer, and spend five minutes doing something quite different, getting a coffee, checking your email, and clearing your mind of the story entirely. Then come back to it and treat it as though you haven't seen it before.

As you read through the story, imagine that you don't know the next point, and work out what your next question would be. Does the next sentence answer that question? This ability to distance yourself from your work, and put yourself in the position of the audience, is vital for all sorts of jobs. Some artists, when they have been working on a painting for some time, hold it up and look at it in a mirror, which helps to distance it and then to see it as a viewer might.

So a story might be constructed as the answers to some of the following questions:

Intro: Who did what; or What happened? Perhaps When? and Where? might be in this paragraph. Note that in a quirky story, the 'where' is not important.

Para 2:   This is the hardest one to work out. If you are reporting an accident or fire, you will probably have told us about casualties in the intro. If you haven't, it must be here. If you are reporting a political event, then the implications for the future might be the next most important point. In many cases this second paragraph will answer the questions Why? or How? Or it might simply be 'Good gracious, tell me more ...'

Para 3:   This is where a quote would often appear. This is viewed by most reporters as essential to keep the story lively. But make sure the quote answers the next question your reader would have. It might be 'So what was it like for the people on the bus?' or 'What does this mean for the government?' Beware the 'I was gutted' quote. By this I mean that if a team loses a football match, of course they are gutted. What you need for the quote is why they lost, what they might do next, etc.

After this, the questions will be different for every story. But here are some of the questions your readers might ask:

- Why are you telling me this/what are the implications of this? (significance)
- Are you sure this is right? (source)
- What does the prime minister/Mick Jagger/the granny/the council/the neighbour think about this? (moving the story on, giving it a human context)
- How did this state of affairs come about? (essential background)
- What is going to happen next? (again, moving the story on, significance)
- Where does this fit into the big picture? (if there is one)

SCENARIO 1: BUNBURY PRISON INCIDENT

Below I have set out a news story about some fictional events at an imaginary women's jail. First I have set out the facts in a way that a reporter might have gathered them. Then the news story follows, with a commentary.

PRESS STATEMENT FROM HM PRISON
BUNBURY, BLUNTFORD ROAD LONDON

Following an incident yesterday (Sunday) morning at the prison, five officers from other prisons in London have been drafted in to Bunbury. This is because six of our staff are temporarily off duty following the incident.

An emergency was called at 8.33 am when two inmates barricaded a cell and set fire to a mattress inside it. Two other inmates were held hostage in the cell. Our officers tackled the fire and brought the hostages to safety. The situation was resolved by 9.15 am. But as a result of tackling the fire, three officers are suffering from smoke inhalation, and one from minor burns. Another was punched in the stomach, and in an unrelated incident later yesterday another was bitten by an inmate. The three with smoke inhalation were treated at Whitefields Hospital and have been allowed home.

The others were seen by a doctor on site. The incident happened in the wing where new prisoners are held.

Every prison has a Board of Visitors which monitors conditions and other matters at the jail. The board is made up of local people who do this voluntarily. They have the right to go into the jail and talk to prisoners. You ring Ms Lesley Hershey, chair of Bunbury's Board of Visitors, and she says:

'I visited Bunbury yesterday afternoon and spoke to a number of staff and inmates, including the women who had been held hostage. One of them is not quite 18 years old. I am satisfied that the situation is now calm.

The hostages were terrified during their ordeal and the young one is now in the hospital wing for observation. She is suffering from shock. The hostages told me they thought they were going to die. One of the women had set fire to a mattress. It was a very tricky situation. The prison was simmering afterwards. There were girls shouting out of the windows and the situation could have blown up again. The staff handed it excellently.

It seems that the trouble blew up because one new inmate was not happy about education classes being cancelled and the regime for showers.'

You ring Mr Ed Sharpe, governor of Bunbury, who says:

'Emergencies are rare in prisons. None of the injuries was serious, but when you attend to a fire you get burns and suffer from smoke inhalation. Also one officer was punched, and later another was bitten, so all in all we were six officers down.

Bunbury should have a total of 220 officers, but at present we have 175. Next month eight new staff are joining and 14 new recruits will begin training. The moment we put in place a substantial staff, Bunbury will change significantly and for the better.'

You check your database, and your paper had the following story two weeks ago:

A row has erupted over whether the notorious Bunbury women's prison should be used to remand child offenders. In a report this week, the chief inspector of prisons, Fiona Peyton, said it was 'inexcusable and depressing' that few changes had been made since the jail's last inspection, and called for all girls under 18 to be relocated. Inspectors found that women prisoners, even those that were pregnant or had recently given birth, were unable to shower more than twice a week, while some areas suffered from cockroaches and feral pigeons.

'In our view, girls should not be held in Bunbury,' said Fiona Peyton. 'No assessments of vulnerability and risk were being carried out, the regime was wholly inadequate, staff lacked essential documentation and no work was being done on making sure each inmate had a plan for education and training.

'This inspectorate has repeatedly drawn attention to the deficiencies in the care of girls in prison in general and the situation of young women in Bunbury in particular. It is both inexcusable and depressing that these continue and that it takes an inspection to galvanise those responsible into action.'

Here is a possible news story.

STORY AND QUESTIONS BY IMAGINARY READER

Two terrified inmates, one a teenager, were held hostage in a burning cell at Bunbury Prison on Sunday in a riot over cancelled classes and showers.

Para 1: *All the drama of the incident is in here: and all of the five Ws.*

Two inmates barricaded themselves into a cell, taking two others hostage, and setting fire to a mattress. One of the hostages is 17.

Para 2: *My goodness, who held them hostage? And you say one of the hostages was a teenager?*

Prison officers took control again after 45 minutes, putting the fire out and releasing the two hostages.

Para 3: *Is it still going on then? What happened to the hostages?*

Six prison officers were injured, three from smoke inhalation, one with burns, and one who was punched in the stomach. In an unrelated incident later in the day another officer was bitten by an inmate.

Para 4: *This sounds dangerous. Was anyone hurt?*

Lesley Hershey, chair of the jail's Board of Visitors, said yesterday: 'The hostages were terrified during their ordeal and the younger one is now in the hospital wing for observation. She is suffering from shock. The hostages told me they thought they were going to die.'

Para 5: *Quote (answers the questions: Are the hostages okay? What did they think about it?)*

Ms Hershey said tension was high in the jail after the incident. 'The prison was simmering afterwards. There were girls shouting out of the windows and the situation could have blown up again. The staff handled it excellently.'

Para 6: *So what is it like there now?*

The jail is seriously understaffed, with 175 officers when there should be 220. Ms Hershey said the trouble blew up because one new inmate was not happy about education classes and the regime for showers.

Para 7: Any reason why this happened?

Two weeks ago a row erupted over whether the jail should be used to remand child offenders. In a report then, the chief inspector of prisons, Fiona Peyton, said it was 'inexcusable and depressing' that few changes had been made since Bunbury's previous inspection. She called for all prisoners under 18 to be relocated. Inspectors found that prisoners, even those who were pregnant or had recently given birth, were unable to shower more than twice a week. Some areas were infested with cockroaches and feral pigeons.

Para 8: I seem to remember something about the jail a week or two ago...

'In our view girls should not be held at Bunbury,' Ms Peyton said then. 'No assessments of vulnerability and risk were being carried out, and the regime was wholly inadequate, staff lacked essential documentation and no work was being done on making sure each inmate had plans for education and training.'

Para 9: And wasn't there something about youngsters being there?

In a statement today the jail said five officers from elsewhere in London had been drafted in to cover those temporarily off duty.

Para 10: So how are they managing at the jail now? And what about the future?

Ed Sharpe, governor of Bunbury, said nine new staff were joining this month, and 15 new recruits would begin training. "The moment we put in place a substantial staff, Bunbury will change significantly and for the better.'

SCENARIO 2: UNIVERSITY APPLICATIONS DECLINE

Here is a very different story, covered in most of the nationals. In February 2006, as the deadline passed for applications for university places through UCAS, there were reports and comments about a drop in applications. Here are the main facts:

University and college applications received by the closing date, January 15, were down 3.4 per cent on last year – nearly double the figure which had been predicted by the higher education minister, Bill Rammell.

The drop coincides with an increase in fees next year from £1,175 to £3,000.

English applicants to universities in England – the group hardest hit by top-up fees – were down 4.5 per cent.

Demand grew for maths, chemistry, physics and some engineering degrees. But applications for courses in the arts and humanities, including history and English, fell. Applications for media studies, publicity studies and cinematics also fell.

The figures also suggest a greater fall in applications from middle-class students. They miss out on government grants and university bursaries intended to offset the rise in annual fees.

The National Union of Students, which campaigned against higher fees, said the overall drop showed that fear of debt and confusion about the new system were deterring students.

The president of the NUS, Kat Fletcher, said: 'The drop in applications is extremely worrying, and suggests that top-up fees and the debt they represent is deterring potential students.

'As a society, we could be missing out on thousands of potential doctors, teachers, scientists and engineers because the fear of debt has put them off from going to university and achieving their aspirations. Some students may not have applied because they did not understand what was on offer,' she added.

Rammell said: 'What you might describe as subjects which students see as really non-vocational – like fine art, philosophy, classical studies – have seen big reductions. That's why I say an initial reading of the figures suggests to me that there is some evidence students are choosing subjects they think are more vocationally beneficial. If that's what they are doing, I don't see that as necessarily a bad thing.'

He insisted there is merit in arts courses, but added: 'If students are making a calculation about which degree is going to get them the best job and the best opportunity in life, I see that as being no bad thing.'

Jonathan Wolff, philosophy professor at University College London, said: 'It is a bad mistake to think subjects like philosophy, history and classics do not prepare students for the workplace. There is no better recipe for misery than studying a vocational subject for which one has no vocation – especially when this is compounded with debt.'

Tory higher education spokesman Boris Johnson, who read classics at Oxford, said: 'It is economically illiterate to think subjects like philosophy and classics are not valuable degrees. They greatly develop intellectual powers and employers rate people who have done well in them extremely highly. We should not be saying anything to discourage people from studying great and ancient disciplines.'

Mr Rammell read French and politics at Cardiff University. His remarks were reminiscent of an attack three years ago on studying classics by Charles Clarke, then education secretary.

> Mr Clarke also said it was 'not such a bad thing' if top-up fees altered subject trends and singled out classics – prompting dons to accuse him of 'pig ignorance'.

Looking at all this material, there is no doubt we have a story here. We could start with the drop in applications, which is fine, and this is what some news providers did. For example, the BBC had a straight story on these lines on its website:

> University applications have fallen for the first time in six years, as higher fees are introduced across England.
> Almost 13,000 fewer students have applied for courses starting in September than had applied at this time last year – a fall of 3.4%.
> The National Union of Students blamed the fall on higher tuition fees, where students will pay up to £3,000 a year.

We could go for the quote from Bill Rammell, which takes the story forward, and gives an extra tension. The debate about which university subjects are the best ones to study has been going on for some time, therefore his quote has a consonance. This is what the *Daily Telegraph* did:

> A sharp fall in the number of university applicants wanting to study such 'non-vocational' subjects as history, philosophy, classics and fine art was 'no bad thing', Bill Rammell, the higher education minister, said yesterday.
> He was commenting on statistics showing that the impending rise in university fees to £3,000 a year had caused the first drop for eight years in the total numbers applying.

Or we can search for the most conflict and tension possible in these facts, and go for the reaction to Rammell. This is what the *Daily Mail* chose to do:

STORY AND QUESTIONS BY IMAGINARY READER

A minister was yesterday accused of being 'economically illiterate' after he appeared to welcome the decline of arts subjects in universities.

Para 1: *Who? What? When? Why (note the intro takes the point with the greatest tension)*

Bill Rammell said it was 'no bad thing' that tripling university tuition fees had deterred students from taking courses such as philosophy, the classics and fine art.

Para 2: *What did he say exactly? And what was he referring to? (note the clear and economical way that essential points are woven in, the tripling of fees and the details of which courses)*

The higher education minister said bumping up fees to £3,000 a year this autumn appeared to have put students off 'really non-vocational' subjects.

Para 3: Did you say tripled? What exactly did he say?

But dons and opposition MPs said he had made a big mistake in attacking 'great and ancient' traditional arts disciplines.

Para 4: So who has attacked him?

Mr Rammell made his comments after Universities and Colleges Admissions Service figures showed that tuition fees are scaring off thousands of students.

Para 5: Why has all this blown up now? What are the facts behind this then?

University applications are down for the first time for six years. Applications received by the closing date on January 15 were down 3.4 per cent on last year – nearly double the figure predicted by Mr Rammell.

Para 6: Not a major answer to the next question, but an interesting bit of detail showing an even greater fall.

English applicants to universities in England – the group hardest hit by top-up fees – were down 4.5 per cent.

Paras 7–10: So what are the facts about this fall then?

But the fall, which student leaders described as 'extremely worrying' – masked wide disparities in different subjects.

Demand grew for maths, chemistry, physics and some engineering degrees. But applications for courses in the arts and humanities, including history and English, fell.

Applications for so-called 'Mickey Mouse' courses, such as media studies, publicity studies and cinematics, also dipped as higher costs concentrated students' minds on the career value of different subjects.

Mr Rammell, who read French at Cardiff University, said: 'What you might describe as subjects which students see as really non-vocational – like fine art, philosophy, classical studies – have seen big reductions. That's why I say an initial reading of the figures suggests to me that there is some evidence students are choosing subjects they think are more vocationally beneficial. If that's what they are doing, I don't see that as necessarily a bad thing.'

Paras 11–12: What exactly did he say then?

He insisted there is merit in arts courses, but added: 'If students are making a calculation about which degree is going to get them the best job and the best opportunity in life, I see that as being no bad thing.'

His remarks were reminiscent of an attack three years ago on studying classics by Charles Clarke, then education secretary.

Paras 13–14: this seems to ring a bell: didn't someone else say something like this before?

Mr Clarke also said it was 'not such a bad thing' if top-up fees altered subject trends and singled out classics – prompting dons to accuse him of 'pig ignorance'.

Jonathan Wolff, philosophy professor at University College London,

Para 15–18: So what is all this about attacks then?

said: 'It is a bad mistake to think subjects like philosophy, history and classics do not prepare students for the workplace.'

'There is no better recipe for misery than studying a vocational subject for which one has no vocation – especially when this is compounded with debt,' he added.

Tory higher education spokesman Boris Johnson, who read classics at Oxford, said: 'It is economically illiterate to think subjects like philosophy and classics are not valuable degrees.

'They greatly develop intellectual powers and employers rate people who have done well in them extremely highly. We should not be saying anything to discourage people from studying great and ancient disciplines.'

The figures also suggest a greater fall in applications from middle-class students. They miss out on government grants and university bursaries intended to offset the rise in annual fees from £1,175 to £3,000.

Para 19: Another interesting point for Daily Mail *readers.*

SUGGESTION FOR DISCUSSION

Look at 'straight' news stories in national newspapers or on websites. Read the intro and try to imagine what is the next thing you would want to know. Is that in the next paragraph? Carry on doing this as you read the story. Does the story follow the next question that you would have in your mind at the end of each paragraph? If it doesn't, try to work out why not. Note that this approach will not always work with humorous or quirky stories.

STRUCTURE PART 3: AVOIDING NARRATIVE

When a news story is based on a single new event, such as a crime, a takeover bid, or a celeb wedding announcement, then it is not difficult to see what the story is, and how to follow the inverted pyramid principle.

But often reporters are confronted with a chain of events. This is particularly the case when reporting from courts, and can also happen when a complicated story has been going on for some time, such as with a protracted argument over a planning application, or a long-running political controversy.

If you listen to a court case lasting a day or so, you might hear quite a long story, say about a young man collecting his girlfriend from her home, going to a club, taking a few drugs, having a big row, leaving the club unexpectedly, driving off at speed pursued by police, being critically injured in a car crash, and dying later in hospital. As well as all these events, there might then be material from the hospital, and then the inquest, which the reporter attends. Sometimes the inquest might have still more newsworthy material: the family perhaps is not satisfied about the police actions, or perhaps about the hospital treatment.

Confronted with all this, it can be hard for inexperienced journalists to see the wood for the trees. They get quite a newsy intro, but then can't work out what to do next, so they go back to the beginning and tell the story in a chronological way:

> A young electrician was fatally injured when his car crashed into a lamp-post while he was being chased by police through Northampton, an inquest was told yesterday.
> John Smith collected his girlfriend Jane Brown from her home earlier that evening ...

This is not the best way to write a news story. The intro is fine, but the second paragraph has a pedestrian, story-book feel to it. It doesn't hold the reader's attention, and is likely to be read only by people who are already interested in these events because they know some of the people involved.

To get readers to stay interested in such a story for its own sake, the second paragraph needs almost as much drama as the first, and the third almost as much as the second, and so on.

> A young electrician was fatally injured when his car crashed into a lamp-post while he was being chased by police through Northampton, an inquest was told yesterday.
>
> John Smith had been pursued by police after he was seen driving at 60 miles per hour through the centre of the town in August last year, PC Peter Thomas said in court.
>
> Mr Smith's car hit a lamp-post in Long Lane, spun round twice, and came to rest against a tree, PC Thomas said.
>
> Mr Smith's girlfriend Jane Brown told the court that they had had a row shortly after they arrived at Dampers Club in Short Street that evening ...

Inquests and crown courts often provide stories rather like this. There might be quite a long chain of events, culminating in a moment of high drama. This moment of high drama will almost certainly be the intro to the story.

SCENARIO 1: THE *HAMLET* PLOT

An example I use with my students is Shakespeare's tragedy *Hamlet;* a summary of the plot follows:

> The chain of events begins before the play opens, with the sudden death of old King Hamlet. His brother Claudius becomes king, and soon after the funeral, marries the widowed Queen Gertrude.
>
> Even within the confines of a narrative, Shakespeare begins '*in medias res*': he starts at a moment of drama on the castle battlements, with the appearance of the dead king's ghost. The ghost tells Hamlet that he was murdered by Claudius. Hamlet, already gloomy about his father's death and about his mother's speedy remarriage, is made even more gloomy because honour demands that he avenge his father. Unable to deal with all this, he pretends to be mad, and has a row with his girlfriend Ophelia.
>
> A couple of chums from university, Rosencrantz and Guildenstern, turn up, as do some travelling actors, whom Hamlet persuades to enact a play in which a king is killed by his brother. The play infuriates Claudius, who rushes out of the room, thus proving his guilt.
>
> Hamlet is summoned to see Gertrude, has a row with her, and hearing a noise behind a curtain, runs his sword through it, believing he is killing Claudius and avenging his father. Unfortunately it is a boring old courtier called Polonius, Ophelia's father.
>
> Even in those days, and even if you are a prince, murder is serious, so Claudius sends Hamlet to England with the two friends from university, on a pretext of getting him out of the country while the scandal dies down. Parallel to all this, Fortinbras, Prince of Norway, marches through Denmark with an army planning to wage war over a tiny and worthless piece of land.
>
> It turns out that Claudius arranged the trip to England not to help Hamlet live down the scandal, but to get him murdered. Suspecting this, Hamlet swaps a letter and poor Rosencrantz and Guildenstern are murdered instead.

Things go very rapidly from bad to worse. Laertes, Polonius's son, wants to avenge his father, Ophelia goes mad and drowns herself, and Hamlet returns from England and interrupts her funeral by rowing with Laertes in the open grave.

Claudius arranges an after-dinner fencing match between Hamlet and Laertes, but unbeknown to the prince, it is a murder plot. Laertes has a fencing foil which not only does not have a guard, but is tipped with poison. To make doubly sure, Claudius arranges a glass of poisoned wine for Hamlet.

Everything goes dreadfully wrong. Hamlet is wounded by the poisoned foil, swaps it and wounds Laertes, and realizing it is poisoned, stabs the king as well. Gertrude drinks the poison meant for Hamlet, and a tedious courtier called Osric is also killed with the poisoned foil.

The only people of any significance left alive are Hamlet's friend Horatio and Prince Fortinbras, who fortuitously marches back in at the last moment to become king.

So the *Elsinore Bugle* has quite a story on its hands for the following morning's edition. It is not difficult to get a good intro:

The entire royal family were killed in a bloodbath at Elsinore Castle last night ...

But then, because the story is so complicated, often inexperienced students want to go back to the beginning and start telling us about the old king and the ghost and so on. That is not the best way to do it. A good classic news story would keep focused on the main news point, weaving in bits of background as necessary. It would keep driving forward, rather than going back to the beginning.

Shakespeare's play takes about four hours to perform and goes through from very near the beginning of the chain of events to the end. The experienced chief reporter on the *Elsinore Bugle* constructs a news story which gives all that information, but stays in the here and now of the fateful day, diving back from time to time to scoop up bits of background, such as explaining what happened to Polonius, Ophelia, etc.

The point about the news story is that the reporter imposes her own order on it, the order of drama, without any constraints of time or place. The version of this news story that follows is only one way to do it. There are several other possibilities, but this is one that might be put out on an agency wire, or on the front of the next day's paper:

The King, the Queen and Prince Hamlet were killed last night at Elsinore Palace in a sword fight believed to have been sparked by a row over succession to the throne.

Para 1: Who: royals; What: killed; Where: palace; When: last night; Why: succession (we don't know this, but it's a likely assumption).

First reports from the bloody scene suggest that King Claudius and Prince Hamlet died from wounds caused by a fencing foil that had lost its guard. But other sources mentioned a palace plot involving poison, and said Queen Gertrude died after drinking poisoned wine.

Para 2: Blimey, all of them? How?

Prince Fortinbras of Norway has been declared King and will speak from the palace balcony this afternoon at 3 pm.

Para 3: Who is in charge now?

The carnage ends the troubled house of Hamlet, which has been beset by rumours about a dispute between King Claudius and Hamlet.

Para 4: What's it about then? (significance, interpretation)

Horatio, a courtier and friend of Hamlet, said there had been 'accidental judgments, casual slaughters, deaths put on by cunning, and forc'd cause'.

Para 5: Quote: notice that the quote is not just a comment, but tells us about some of the dramas.

A scene of devastation greeted Norwegian Prince Fortinbras when he arrived late last night after winning a battle against Poland.

Para 6: 'Picture', plus tying up loose end about Fortinbras.

As well as the three royals, two courtiers died last night from sword wounds. They were Osric and Laertes, whose father died mysteriously last month.

Para 7: Answering likely immediate rumours about five bodies.

Sources say the bloodstained bodies were found strewn in the great hall amid the wreckage of a sumptuous banquet.

Para 8: More picture.

Investigators today began the grisly task of sifting through the evidence for clues about an evening which started with feasting and ended with five violent deaths.

Para 9: Keeping story up to date – focusing on now.

Last night's dinner was said by insiders to be an attempt to heal the rift between the King and his nephew. It is known that the prince was unhappy about his mother's marriage to her brother-in-law so soon after the sudden death of her first husband, King Hamlet.

Para 10: Essential background, made immediate by references to banquet.

Insiders say that in an attempt to placate Hamlet, the King had named the prince as his heir, and earlier yesterday evening had presented him with a valuable pearl.

Para 11: Background but still related to last night.

The prince's friends said they and Hamlet himself were worried about plans for an after-dinner fencing match, in which the prince was drawn against Laertes.

Para 12: Essential background.

They said the young courtier had plotted against Hamlet, whom he held responsible for the suicide last week of his sister Ophelia. Her name had been romantically linked to the prince's.

Para 13–14: Ditto and again essential background about Ophelia.

Since King Hamlet's death on September 20 there have been rumours that key personnel have disappeared, and ghosts have been sighted.

Aides say King Fortinbras, fresh from success in battle, is keen to distance himself from the Hamlets. Insiders say he believed that Prince Hamlet had been wavering and undecided since his father's death, although he paid tribute to him in a statement: 'He was likely, had he been put on, to have proved most royally.'

Para 15: Again focusing on now, plus quote.

The Prince, who was not with the royal party at his mother's marriage to King Claudius, left university without a degree, broke off his romance and embarked on travels to England, only to return within days.

Para 16: Essential background ... story could go on for many more pages if necessary: more background about Claudius, etc. but always best interspersed with material about last night.

The possibilities for the background stories inside the paper are endless. Depending on how many reporters the *Bugle* has and how much time is available, they would include profiles of the royals (The Troubled Hamlets; Prince without a Role), certainly a profile of Fortinbras, the new leader (Action Man King), a chronology of recent events in the royal household, interviews with staff, profiles of investigating officers and so on. There would have to be obituaries, which would have already been prepared, and a leading article. Tabloids might have bought up some of the palace staff. There might also be a narrative version of the front-page news story.

Newspapers nowadays are keen on this retelling of the same events in a chronological form on an inside page (It was a busy day at the palace yesterday afternoon as staff prepared for an evening banquet. The dinner was the grandest since the marriage ...).

Have a look at the story again, placed alongside Shakespeare's narrative version (Figure 6.1). The lines linking the point in the narrative version with the same point in the news story show that the first half of the news version is

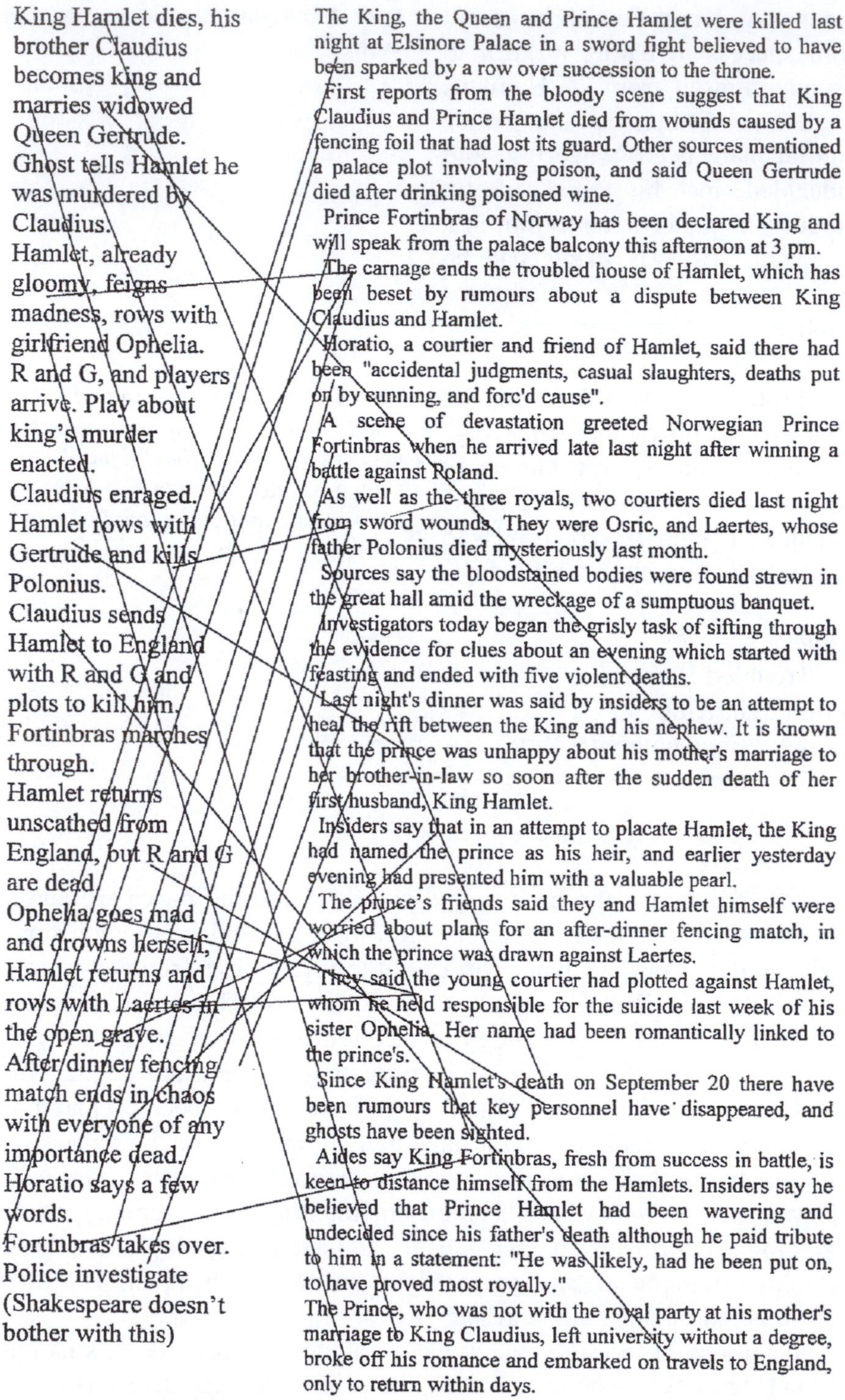

King Hamlet dies, his brother Claudius becomes king and marries widowed Queen Gertrude. Ghost tells Hamlet he was murdered by Claudius. Hamlet, already gloomy, feigns madness, rows with girlfriend Ophelia. R and G, and players arrive. Play about king's murder enacted. Claudius enraged. Hamlet rows with Gertrude and kills Polonius. Claudius sends Hamlet to England with R and G and plots to kill him. Fortinbras marches through. Hamlet returns unscathed from England, but R and G are dead. Ophelia goes mad and drowns herself. Hamlet returns and rows with Laertes in the open grave. After dinner fencing match ends in chaos with everyone of any importance dead. Horatio says a few words. Fortinbras takes over. Police investigate (Shakespeare doesn't bother with this)

The King, the Queen and Prince Hamlet were killed last night at Elsinore Palace in a sword fight believed to have been sparked by a row over succession to the throne.

First reports from the bloody scene suggest that King Claudius and Prince Hamlet died from wounds caused by a fencing foil that had lost its guard. Other sources mentioned a palace plot involving poison, and said Queen Gertrude died after drinking poisoned wine.

Prince Fortinbras of Norway has been declared King and will speak from the palace balcony this afternoon at 3 pm.

The carnage ends the troubled house of Hamlet, which has been beset by rumours about a dispute between King Claudius and Hamlet.

Horatio, a courtier and friend of Hamlet, said there had been "accidental judgments, casual slaughters, deaths put on by cunning, and forc'd cause".

A scene of devastation greeted Norwegian Prince Fortinbras when he arrived late last night after winning a battle against Poland.

As well as the three royals, two courtiers died last night from sword wounds. They were Osric, and Laertes, whose father Polonius died mysteriously last month.

Sources say the bloodstained bodies were found strewn in the great hall amid the wreckage of a sumptuous banquet.

Investigators today began the grisly task of sifting through the evidence for clues about an evening which started with feasting and ended with five violent deaths.

Last night's dinner was said by insiders to be an attempt to heal the rift between the King and his nephew. It is known that the prince was unhappy about his mother's marriage to her brother-in-law so soon after the sudden death of her first husband, King Hamlet.

Insiders say that in an attempt to placate Hamlet, the King had named the prince as his heir, and earlier yesterday evening had presented him with a valuable pearl.

The prince's friends said they and Hamlet himself were worried about plans for an after-dinner fencing match, in which the prince was drawn against Laertes.

They said the young courtier had plotted against Hamlet, whom he held responsible for the suicide last week of his sister Ophelia. Her name had been romantically linked to the prince's.

Since King Hamlet's death on September 20 there have been rumours that key personnel have disappeared, and ghosts have been sighted.

Aides say King Fortinbras, fresh from success in battle, is keen to distance himself from the Hamlets. Insiders say he believed that Prince Hamlet had been wavering and undecided since his father's death although he paid tribute to him in a statement: "He was likely, had he been put on, to have proved most royally."

The Prince, who was not with the royal party at his mother's marriage to King Claudius, left university without a degree, broke off his romance and embarked on travels to England, only to return within days.

Figure 3   Narrative Versus News

very heavily dependent on material from the end of the narrative. And as the story progresses, the reporter has taken care to weave in bits from the narrative, while keeping the news story driving forward with points about the banquet, the succession, the police investigation and so on. At no stage is the forward thrust of the story held up by a whole paragraph of background. The background is of course all essential, but it is woven in as the story moves forward.

SCENARIO 2: THE *OTHELLO* PLOT

Have a look at the story of Othello set out below. This, like all Shakespeare's tragedies, would have been a great news story in its day. It has political significance, (governor dies in mysterious circumstances), and is also a great human interest story, with celebs, sex and race issues.

> The story begins in Venice, after Othello, a top-ranking soldier employed by the Venetian state, has secretly married Desdemona, daughter of Brabantio, a Venetian senator. Othello is considerably older than his new wife, and is black. Brabantio is furious and disowns his daughter.
>
> Iago, a lieutenant in Othello's army, dislikes his general and plots with Roderigo (a disappointed suitor of Desdemona). Othello is sent to the Venetian colony of Cyprus where he becomes governor to repel a threatened Turkish invasion. Desdemona follows him. Othello promotes another lieutenant, Michael Cassio, over Iago, making him even more disgruntled.
>
> Iago suggests to Othello that Desdemona has been unfaithful to him with Cassio. He engineers a drunken brawl for which Cassio is blamed and is therefore dismissed by Othello. Cassio appeals to Desdemona, who pleads for him with Othello, thus convincing her husband that Cassio is her lover.
>
> Iago, through his wife Emilia, who is Desdemona's maid, acquires a treasured handkerchief from Desdemona, gives it to Cassio, and thus uses it to convince Othello that there is an affair. In a jealous rage, Othello comes to Desdemona in their bedroom and strangles her. As members of the entourage break into the room, Emilia reveals to Othello that he has been duped by Iago. The latter, furious, murders his own wife, and is wounded by Othello.
>
> The general, tormented by remorse, is disarmed and left alone with his innocent dead wife. He has another knife hidden in the chamber and with it he kills himself.

CONSTRUCTING YOUR STORY

First decide what paper you are writing for: for a paper in Cyprus the most important Who of the story will be Othello, who recently arrived on the island as governor. For a Venetian paper, the Who might be Desdemona – a young noblewoman who was born and brought up in the city. For Venetians, Othello, who is a mercenary soldier, is probably less important.

For the Cyprus paper then, the intro might be something on the lines of:

General Othello killed himself after murdering his young Venetian bride at their home last night, police said.

This intro covers the Who, What, Where, and When, but does not address the question Why. It is quite short, but since the answer to Why, the jealousy point and Iago's role in the story are quite complicated, it might be better not to clutter the intro trying to explain them.

So the first question your readers will have will be Why?

Police believe that Othello had become convinced that his wife was having an affair and killed her in a fit of jealousy.

The story will then continue with more up-to-the-minute details of the events, weaving in background about Cassio and covering essentials about who is now in charge of the island.

For a Venetian paper (assuming news travels fast) the intro might be something like this:

Desdemona, daughter of senator Brabantio, was murdered in Cypus last night by her husband, the Moorish general Othello, who then cut his own throat, police said.

This is 26 words, so depending how much of a well-known IT-girl Desdemona was, the phrase 'daughter of senator Brabantio' could be left for further down the story. This story for Venetian readers would then focus on Desdemona, her elopement, quote from her father, and so on.

SUGGESTION FOR DISCUSSION

I get students to do an exercise, basing a news story on something they know as a narrative. I tend not to let them use fairy tales, although some of them, such as Snow White and the Seven Dwarves, make excellent news stories. They often base their stories on films, so we get all sorts of stories for the *Inter-Galactic Times* based on the Star Wars films, and so on. I don't let them do the exercise about the film *Titanic*: that was a huge news story long before it was a narrative.

The important point for student journalists to think about is that confronted with a chain of events, they can and should impose their own order on the material. Remember to rearrange all the elements in the order of the most dramatic down to the least dramatic, rather than sticking to the chronological order.

7
OTHER NEWS WRITING
MODELS FOR INTROS

The more dramatic, tragic or newsworthy a story is, the better it is to stick to the classic inverted pyramid approach described earlier in Chapter 4. Any other model is always going to seem slightly feature-like, and very often slightly jokey. Often of course this is fine, and there are many cases where the whole point of the story is to tell it in a rather relaxed way. This approach is especially good for amusing human interest or quirky stories.

DROP INTRO, DELAYED DROP

Some different ways of starting a news story have been given slightly odd names by older hacks, though perhaps younger reporters do not use such expressions as those above. These two terms mean roughly the same thing: that the main point of the story, the one that in a straight treatment would be in the first paragraph, is left until further down. I shall call this model the delayed drop.

This treatment is almost always going to introduce jokiness into the story, so the first thing to stress is that it is most definitely not suitable for any kind of story which involves bad news:

> It was a beautiful sunny July day and Janet Frost was sitting in her kitchen reading the paper when there was a knock on the door. Little did she know that three murderers armed with machetes were about to burst into her home …

This is in extremely poor taste. For the same reason, any kind of humorous pun or double meaning headline is not at all suitable for a tragic story. It is sometimes hard to convince young reporters of this, but you only have to study the tabloids to see that although they are full of clever punning or jokey headlines on the sports pages and over light celebrity or human interest stories, these treatments are simply not used for serious human tragedies.

There is a good case for saying that a quirky lifestyle or celebrity story benefits a great deal from a delayed drop. A straight dramatic news intro on what is essentially an unimportant story can look overly portentous. Here is a classic example of a delayed drop from the *Daily Express:*

> Wild boars can be intimidating creatures. They wield razor-sharp tusks, and weigh in at 440 lb – and have put one alarmed village under siege.
> The small community is reeling after 100 of the snarling beasts were freed from a farm by animal rights extremists.

This works very well. The story could have had a straight intro, but the reporter has chosen to home in first on the boars, making sure the reader knows exactly how terrifying they are, and then we get the 'clunk' of the village under siege. Note all the listen-to-me words: intimidating, wield, razor-sharp tusks, alarmed, siege.

Clunk is an expression I use in teaching feature writing: when the reader is brought up sharply at the end of a sentence or paragraph with a surprise word, phrase or news point. One of the best clunks I have found was in the *Financial Times* on a feature which was certainly not jokey – the clunk here was a very nasty surprise:

> My namesake lives in Florida. His photograph and essential details are on a state-sponsored website telling the world about his exclusive lifestyle.
> Yet he himself has no telephone number or e-mail address. He writes letters on lined paper with a special floppy biro. My namesake is on Death Row.

There is a particular kind of delayed drop when the writer uses a pronoun at first, so we don't know exactly who they are talking about:

> In the rarefied world of poetry, she is an unusual beast: a critical success with a popular readership. Carol Ann Duffy reconfirmed her reputation for both last night … (*Independent*)

Or:

> They are the reigning premiership champions and, with 15 games left to play, they are romping away with this season's title. But yesterday Chelsea collected a new though rather unwelcome accolade by reporting a £140 million financial loss, the largest in football history. (*Guardian*)

These both work well. In the second case we assume every reader who would be interested in this story already knows which club we are talking about. In the first case, the headline made it clear anyway. I am not all that fond of this style, perhaps simply because I thought it was rather clever when I was a trainee a long while ago, so it seems to me to be rather old hat now. But there is no doubt that in both cases these intros give some variety to the writing in the paper. The columnist Nick Cohen claims that when he was a reporter he sometimes used to drop the intro so far down, to the last paragraph in fact, that it was removed from the story entirely. This is not recommended.

THE SLOW BURNER

This is another expression used by older journalists, and generally refers to a story where the writer gives us quite a lot of information, and then gets to the actual news point several paragraphs in. There is a gradual build-up, possibly humorous, to the main point.

There were good examples of several ways of doing this when most newspapers ran a story about a parrot that was such a good mimic that it revealed to its owner that his live-in girlfriend had had an affair. The embarrassment of blurting out the wrong name at an intimate moment is something many of us fear, but the extra twist to this story was that it was the parrot that blurted out the wrong name. The *Sun* used a straight intro:

> Cheated Chris Taylor found out his girlfriend was two-timing him when his pet parrot kept blurting out her lover's name.

The whole package was enlivened with a brilliant headline: POLLY SPILLER and a bubble added to the picture of the parrot saying 'Who's a prettier boy then?' The page, with the headline and caption, worked very well.

But the story was a cracking example of one that could benefit from a slow burner approach, and this is what several other papers chose:

> As Ziggy the parrot's owner enjoyed a cuddle on the settee with live-in lover Suzy Collins, the chatty bird sensed the moment to perform his party piece.
> 'I love you, Gary,' squawked the African Grey in a perfect imitation of Miss Collins's voice.
> The trouble was that his owner's name is not Gary, but Chris Taylor.
> And when he saw Miss Collins's embarrassed reaction, Mr Taylor realised she had been having an affair. (*Daily Mail*)

This is an excellent approach. The reporter has added to the humour by personalizing the parrot, suggesting it was deliberately and proudly producing its mimicry. With plenty of listen-to-me words (cuddle, chatty, party piece, squawk) the story is very lively, and brings us down with a lovely clunk at the end of the third paragraph when all is revealed.

The Times went for an even longer slow burner:

> When Chris Taylor's best friend repeatedly mentioned the name Gary, his suspicions were aroused. He didn't know a Gary.
>
> And when the best friend made slurpy kissing noises every time he heard the name Gary on television, Chris wondered if Ziggy was trying to tell him something about some other pretty boy. The penny dropped when, one romantic evening as Mr Taylor cuddled his girlfriend Suzy Collins on the sofa, Ziggy blurted out: 'I love you Gary.'
>
> What gave the game away was that Ziggy spoke the fatal phrase in Ms Collins's voice. Even by the standards of African Grey parrots, Ziggy is a mimic and a half, and from his cage in the corner he had heard every bill and coo of a secret love affair.
>
> A chill ran down Mr Taylor's spine. He turned to Suzy, whose cheeks had flushed to beetroot …

This is a very funny story. It builds up to the news point by telling us about the relationship between Chris and his 'best friend' who is not identified until the end of the third sentence as a parrot. The humanizing of the parrot again adds to the humour, and this is especially brought out by the word 'blurted'. Puns through the story add to the humour – the 'bill and coo' of the love affair, and later when the couple row we hear that 'feathers flew'.

NARRATIVE STYLE

A slightly different take on the slow burner is a story that is basically written in a narrative way. Look at this example from the *Daily Mail*:

> As last orders neared, the doctors and nurses enjoying a boozy birthday party at the pub had no worries about how they would get home.
>
> Their transport had been booked and it was only a short stagger from the bar to the waiting 'taxi'.
>
> But their choice of vehicle left other drinkers shocked. Waiting outside The Swan in Ironbridge, Shropshire, at 11 pm was an ambulance.
>
> At the end of a five-hour drinking session, about half a dozen of the group of merry hospital medics piled into the back and were driven away.
>
> Yesterday the ambulance's two-man crew faced an investigation …

The story went on with quotes from people in the pub, a patients' group, the ambulance service and the hospital trust. It could have been written straight, but it is a funny quirky story, and the narrative treatment brings out all the humour, and brilliantly puts the reader in the place of the witnesses in the pub. We get the picture of the pub, the lively party, and then, just as surprising as it must have been for onlookers, the arrival of the ambulance. Note also the alliteration: boozy birthday, short stagger, merry medics. A straight version would lose the humour, would not put us in the position of the onlookers, and would possibly seem overly self-righteous.

Here is another good example, also from the *Daily Mail*. Again it is a quirky story, which works very well in this treatment:

Karla Anthony was thrilled with her new pencil case and couldn't wait to show her friends at school.

The eight-year-old used her pocket money to buy it from WH Smith and was particularly fond of the pink bunny with a bow tie emblazoned across the front.

But when her teachers saw it, they banned Karla from bringing the case to school again – because the rabbit was the logo for *Playboy* magazine.

The incident has caused a stand-off between the school and Karla's parents …

This 'once-upon-a-time' method works particularly well here because it is an odd little story, and because it is about a child.

REFLECTIVE/INTERPRETATIVE INTRO

A slightly different model is the reflective intro, which starts with some analysis or reflection on the implications of something, rather than the actual news point. This kind of intro is often found in the *Guardian* and the *Independent*. There may be lots of reasons for this. Both papers are strong on interpretation, wanting to give readers the context and significance of events. Both papers are strong on writing, and tend to give reporters more leeway in their writing than perhaps the *Daily Telegraph* does. Possibly both papers believe that more of their readers have read news online, or watched TV or listened to the radio, so they know the main news points already.

Here are some examples of stories about the end of a *Celebrity Big Brother* series.

Celebrity Big Brother was won last night by the only non-celebrity in the house. Chantelle Houghton, an office temp and Paris Hilton lookalike, won the public vote to take top prize in the Channel 4 show. (*Daily Mail*)

Celebrity Big Brother was won last night by Chantelle Houghton, a 21-year-old model and office temp from Essex, who had been placed in the house by Channel 4 as a 'fake' star. (*Daily Telegraph* front page picture caption/write-off)

Despite howls of protest from unbelievers and high-brow types, the delicious freak-fest known as Celebrity Big Brother has become the kind of entertainment event that is impossible to ignore. (*Daily Telegraph* inside page, by TV critic)

You really couldn't make it up: Chantelle, the nobody who managed to convince the other Celebrity Big Brother contestants that she really was a somebody, survived last night to win the Channel 4 reality TV show. (*The Times*)

DIPPY Chantelle Houghton is set to make a fortune after winning Celebrity Big Brother last night.
The fake celebrity and Paris Hilton lookalike beat ten genuine stars to scoop the title. (*Sun*)

First came the celebrities who were famous for being famous. Now, thanks to Chantelle Houghton, we have a celebrity who is famous for not being famous. (*Independent*)

The Doctor Frankensteins from Endemol really did it this time. With acrylic hair extensions crashing against her waist, a super thick layer of borrowed bronzer, and her ever-present sparkly toothed grin, Chantelle Houghton left the Celebrity Big Brother house in triumph last night. She beat the genuine celebrities and fulfilled the most salient of Warholian prophesies: that everyone one day will be famous for 15 minutes. (*Guardian*)

There is a problem for almost every newspaper in covering this story (apart from the *Financial Times* which didn't cover it, and we presume its readers didn't expect it to do so). The tabloids must assume that a very large proportion of their readers will know what happened, so they need to move the story on from merely reporting Chantelle's win. This is presumably why the *Sun* went for the point about how much she stands to earn by winning. There was a fantastic picture of her in a shiny cream micro-dress which matched her blonde hair, so many papers would have chosen that picture for the front, regardless of what value they were going to place on the story.

The *Daily Telegraph* used it with a two-sentence caption which reported the story in a straightforward way. Almost all the other papers chose to highlight the point that she was the only non-celebrity in what had been billed as a celebrity programme. The *Daily Mail, The Times* and the *Independent* all highlighted this point, with a nice tension between the celebrity/non-celebrity, famous/not famous, nobody/somebody.

The *Guardian* chose to put the story, also with a big picture, in its Column Five on page one, its space for an off-beat piece of writing. This intro uses a delayed drop, but not in the more usual sense of telling us further down what actually happened, but rather giving us some interpretation. It is assumed that the readers have quite a lot of knowledge about all this. It is assumed that the readers know that the production company which makes *Big Brother* is Endemol. Then there is the description of Chantelle, with a plethora of listen-to-me words: acrylic, crashing, borrowed bronzer (note the alliteration in both cases), sparkly, triumph. Then at the end of that long sentence we get the point that she won. And then comes another reflective point in the reference to Andy Warhol. The piece manages to be lively and sharp, because of the description and the use of language, while at the same time being interpretative.

REPORTAGE

In August 2005 Channel 4 ran an investigation into the best and worst places to live in Britain. Hull came out worst and Nottingham second worst. There was also at that time a lot of publicity about the rate of gun crime in Nottingham. Not surprisingly the people of Nottingham were none too happy about this, and the lively *Evening Post* took the chance to do a bit of campaigning. They sent a reporter to talk to the huge influx of fans arriving for the Test match at Trent Bridge.

There was a straight write-off on the front:

Nottingham – what a great city! That's the verdict of fans flocking to the Ashes Test at Trent Bridge.

Inside was a two-page spread with vox pops, lots of photos and a long descriptive piece about the fans, giving the background to the controversy. It is a piece of reportage and a first-person column rolled into one:

The eager horde swarmed over Trent Bridge. Fortified by fried breakfasts, they spilled from local bars – Casa, the Southbank, and the Trent Bridge Inn.
There were soldiers, men in gorilla suits, sudden blooms of Hawaiian shirts.
There were dozens of Aussies in day-glo T-shirts bearing unrepeatable messages of 'encouragement' for their countrymen.
Yet none of the happy band making its way to the Fourth Test seemed to be in body armour.
Not did the cars kangarooing ponderously towards Notts County Cricket Club's famous old ground boast bulletproof glass or a police escort. Were they taking a risk in a 'gun crime' city?
With the exception of Kingston-upon-Hull, this is after all, the 'worst place to live in the United Kingdom'.

The first three paragraphs give a lively picture of the stream of fans, and then the piece gets into sarcastic mood, making jokes about body armour and bulletproof glass. This tone probably fits exactly the views of many of the readers, who must have been very irritated about the mud-slinging the city suffered. Note also all the listen-to-me words: eager, horde, spilled, gorilla, blooms. Also the alliteration of fortified and fried, cars kangarooing, boast bulletproof. Writing good reportage is extremely difficult, and since it is generally used in feature writing, is beyond the scope of this book. But note especially that good reportage is not about sprinkling extra adjectives around. The best reportage is when the colour comes from the verbs and the nouns, the actual nuts and bolts of the meaning, rather than from the descriptive words. This is discussed in more detail in Chapter 9.

Note all the telling verbs: swarmed, fortified, spilled, kangarooing, boast. And all the telling nouns: horde, blooms, soldiers, gorilla suits, happy band.

THE 'SCENE' INTRO

I use this expression when teaching feature writing to students, to describe what is now the most common way to get into a feature. The writer describes the home and surroundings of the person she is profiling, or the detail of the ballet class for a piece about young dancers, or what it is actually like to be in Antarctica. Sometimes the reporter was not actually present at the scene, but through an interview describes, say, a decisive moment in someone's life. This method often work very well, although sometimes it is used when the scene described is too far removed from the actual piece: a scene describing the liberation of Auschwitz to start a piece about Nazi art looting seems to me to be rather cheap.

Here is a brilliant example from the *Daily Mail*:

> Trapped 4,000 ft up a freezing Spanish mountain for six days, Paul Beck was deter-mined to survive.
>
> And after his rescue yesterday, the 33-year-old told how he cheated death by eating raw oats, dry rice and powdered chocolate – and by drinking his own urine.
>
> He spent five nights in sub-zero temperatures and Spanish police said his survival was a miracle.

The scene part of the story is simply the first paragraph. It has got every-thing in there: the dramatic facts of the event, the drama, the human element, and a 'picture' of the scene. And it is only 17 words, three of which are telling dramatic verbs: trapped, was determined and survive.

The second paragraph goes straight back into a conventional reporting mode, but again notice how lively it is, with the indirect quote, the telling detail of what he had to eat (it is hard to imagine eating dry rice) and the clunk of drinking his urine. How much duller the first paragraph would have been as:

> A British man survived for six days in freezing conditions high up a mountain.

FIRST-PERSON PIECES

First-person pieces which are actually news stories are not all that common. Papers tend to use them when a reporter has been an eyewitness to some dra-matic event, perhaps in a war zone or at the scene of a natural disaster. Local papers also use them for all sorts of featurish stories. For example, a reporter will be sent to a speed dating evening or a circus training session. These stories are generally much less structured and the reporter is given much more freedom than with a conventional news story. The *Evening Post* example above is a first-person piece.

IDEAS FOR FURTHER DISCUSSION

In your reading of newspapers and magazines, note stories – and in particu-lar intros – that do not conform to the classic model described in earlier chapters. See whether they fit into any of the models outlined in this chapter, or perhaps form an entirely different category. If you find a new one, please email me at City University! (a.r.mckane@city.ac.uk)

ACCURACY

CHECK, CHECK AND CHECK

Writing a news story sometimes seems to be related to studying mathematics or chemistry. If you add two numbers together, you always get the same answer. It is a fact. If you write up a chemistry experiment, you have to record what happened, you can't embroider it to make your report more interesting. This is why those with some background in science often make very good journalists. They understand the relationship between what they have seen and what they know with what they can then write. When they start learning journalism, some students have to be dissuaded from weaving in a few embellishments to make things more interesting.

Adopting a clear-thinking mathematical approach can be a very good way to ensure that the story is based entirely on the facts you have, not the ones you *wish* you had. So the first thing to be sure about is that you have stuck to the facts you have got. The second is to check them out where possible, especially if they are likely to be disputed. People often ring local papers with allegations of errors or misdeeds perpetrated by councils or other authorities. Often these are not entirely accurate, so they should be checked carefully with the authority.

As you write your story, ask yourself how surprised or incredulous your readers might be at what you are telling them. If you can picture some readers not believing what you have written, then that is a sure sign that you need to check it very carefully. Of course, if you have seen something happen, that's fine, so long as you are sure of what did happen. Most news stories are about things that the reporter did not witness. If possible you need to check with more than one person to confirm that what you are reporting is accurate.

Many news stories are based on what someone said, in which case you need to be very sure that you have heard them correctly. The more outrageous or unusual the quote is, the more careful you need to be. Often you can check with other reporters: it is very common to see reporters checking with each other after a meeting or court case, to make sure they have an accurate record of what was said.

Then you should also check everything else in your story: the names of people, organizations and places, and the facts about a previous event. It is sad but true that if you read a story in local or national newspapers about an area or issue with which you are familiar, you will often notice inaccuracies. The street name will not be quite correct, the person's age will be wrong, the exact locality of the golf club will not be quite right. All this does not help to lift journalism from the low regard in which it is held by the public.

Reporters need to get into the habit of triple-checking everything. A little bell should ring in your head when you get to a place or a name that you might have got wrong. Is it Moreton-in-Marsh, or Moreton-in-the-Marsh? Is the name Anna or Ana, Lesley or Leslie? (This one used to be easier when all Leslies were male and all Lesleys female. This is not now the case.) Is the auction house Christie's or Christies? Is it Jeckyll and Hyde or Jekyll and Hyde? Is the painter Lucien Freud or Lucian Freud? Don't think the internet will always help you, although Google is improving all the time: if you type in Jeckyll and Hyde (which is wrong) it suggests Jekyll and Hyde, which is right. But there are still plenty of references to Jeckyll. Lots of official-looking sites, including art magazines and the like, have Lucian Freud's name spelled wrongly. Even the Queen's website had it wrong at one point, and it also at the time of writing has at least one 'greengrocer's apostrophe' (misplaced apostrophe as in: apple's and pear's). I have written to her on this point, so I hope it will be corrected before this book comes out.

There is no foolproof way of getting things right. Probably a general assumption that you have got it wrong, rather than a general assumption that you have got it right, would help. So develop the habit of checking everything three times. When you write a street name in your notebook, look at it, get it into your head, and then look back at the street sign. When you are writing down someone's name, spell it back to them, even if it is Smith (Smyth? Smythe?) When you transfer the name onto the screen, do the same thing. Look carefully at what you have written, and then back at the correct version in your notebook or on your brief. And look it up again on streetmap.co.uk or on some other site that is likely to be accurate.

When you are checking things on the internet, take great care to assess the site that you are looking at. With more and more blogs out there, as well as sites such as Amazon where people can add their own reviews, there is more and more inaccurate material on the internet. So if you are checking whether it is Newcastle upon or on Tyne, make sure you look at the city's own website or the most authoritative source of information.

You need to be particularly careful about checking facts on film actors and other celebs; the more famous someone is, the more inaccurate information there will be about that person. It takes about six seconds to check things like this, and saves stress and irritation for the subs and news editors. More importantly, you will get a reputation for reliability rather than a reputation for being a liability.

NUMBERS

The single area where reporters make the most mistakes is over numbers. Some of the errors are to do with simply getting a figure wrong, in many cases adding or subtracting a few noughts, or writing kg for gram. Others are to do with making false assumptions. Others are just plain daft.

Figures are important in a story to give weight to the facts, and to back up points. Percentages and ratios are important because they show how something has changed. However, this does not mean that stories should be *about* figures. They should be about people, always, but the figures might show how things have changed for people: more or fewer people moving house, going abroad, being jailed, or whatever.

Whenever you use numbers, check the style book for your publication's rules on writing out the word, using numerals and so on. And if there is no guidance, use your common sense.

GIVE YOUR READER EXACTLY THE AMOUNT OF DETAIL SHE CAN GRASP EASILY

Generally it is good idea to round a figure up or down slightly in the intro, if the number might be difficult for the reader to grasp. So 357,829 might be 'more than 300,000' at first reference. But it is always a good idea to weave in the correct figure further down. This gives your story a solid feeling of detail and accuracy. Remember Dr Johnson's quip: 'Round numbers are always false.'

But don't be too precise for the sake of it. If, for example, 17 out of 58 MPs respond to a survey about the catering service in parliament, that is 29.31034 per cent, but one in three is fine. A good rule-of-thumb here is to count the digits in the number of people you are talking about – here it is two – and then report the ratio in one fewer digit than that. So if you had 100 plus MPs, you could have said 29 per cent. If you had 1,000 you could say 29.3 per cent.

You should always ask yourself how much your reader can take in at one glance. If someone has been in prison 32 years, don't round that down to about 30, because 32 as an idea is perfectly easy to grasp. Use percentages if you have to, but remember that they are harder for your reader to absorb than simple fractions or multiples. There was a piece in the *Scottish Left Review* recently which read:

> Home Office figures have revealed that stop and searches of Asians under new anti-terror laws soared 302 per cent in a year. The total number of stop and searches under counter-terrorism legislation more than doubled from 8,550 to 21,577. Anti-terror searches of blacks rose 230 per cent, from 527 to 1,745, and of whites 118 per cent, from 6,629 to 14,429.

This is all pretty indigestible, and the percentages are particularly hard to grasp. The second sentence, which mentions 'more than doubled', is far easier to follow than the sentences using percentages. The figure of 302 per cent presumably means fourfold, which is much easier to imagine. Try to avoid mixing different kinds of calculations in one story. Don't say a third at one point, and 25 per cent at another. Once you have got your reader in a fraction frame of mind, don't then hit her with a percentage.

ALWAYS GIVE ENOUGH CONTEXT

To make changes clear, you must give a timeframe and a place frame.

> Seven joyriders were killed

means nothing unless you add

> in the past year, in Britain

ALWAYS VISUALIZE WHAT YOU ARE TALKING ABOUT

The Times once ran a story about a bat:

> Britain's largest bat, the greater mouse-eared bat, which was officially declared extinct in the UK 12 years ago, has been rediscovered hibernating in an underground hole in West Sussex. They can weigh up to 30 kg and have ears as long as 3 cm.

The letter writers had a field day:

BAT OUT OF HELL

Sir, Startled to read that a bat weighing in at 30 kg was back, I hastened down to our local supermarket, hoping to arrange 30 bags of sugar in a bat-like formation so that I could properly appreciate this discovery. I left the manager in no doubt that he should take more interest in our wildlife as he escorted me out of his shop. I think he was miffed that even his best turkeys came nowhere near 30 kg; even allowing for the added water content, the best he could offer was a mere 15 kg.

Sir, Why worry about possible terrorist attacks? Should we not be more concerned about the dangers of meeting with a 30 kg bat when it comes out of hibernation?

Sir, Monty, our somewhat overweight yellow labrador, just about weighs 30 kg on a good day. The thought of him equipped with leathery wings and airborne fair boggles the imagination.

Sir, No wonder the mouse-eared bat is hiding in a hole in the ground. It is probably waiting for the results of the airport inquiry to see if there will be a runway big enough to use for take-off.

Sir, My children are struggling with the concept of Santa Claus and flying reindeer. To add 30 kg bats to the night skies is pushing their imagination a little too far.

The bat of course weighed 30g, not 30kg.

On another occasion there was a story about foie gras which asserted that Britain imported 50 million tonnes of it each year. It prompted the following letter:

Sir, I see we imported last year a tonne of foie gras for almost every man, woman and child in the country. I didn't get mine; did someone out there eat two tonnes?

It should have been 50 tonnes of course, not 50 million.

These examples illustrate two useful points. If you have a weight or a length, *always visualize* it. We all know what a kilo of a lot of different substances looks like. Imagine a kilo of sugar. If you held your hands together, palms up, it would just about fit into them. Of course a kilo of lead would be smaller, and of feathers a great deal bigger. But the sugar is an average sort of kilo, similar probably to a kilo of a lot of other things. A kilo of baby, say, might be a little bigger, a kilo of cannabis, being plant material, probably bigger still. If the reporter had pictured the 30 kilos of bat, an error would have been spotted. If you hear in court that someone had a kilo of cannabis in her back pocket, think about it. You have probably misheard. Perhaps it was in a back pack.

The same goes for other physical dimensions. A very tall man is 2 metres high. So if you get a metre-long stick insect in a story, it is either wrong or belongs in the *Guinness Book of Records*.

Know the population of Britain – it is about 59 million. Let's say 60 million for ease of calculation. That means very roughly 10 million people in every decade of life, probably rather fewer. It also means about a million in any year group, and half are female, and half male. So if you get a story about 200,000 school-age girls getting pregnant, that must mean girls aged 12–16. There must be very roughly 2 million girls in that age range in the country. So this figure seems to be about 1 in 10: it can't possibly be right. This is exactly what the writer of the foie gras story should have done, as the letter-writer did.

If you want an arresting image in your story (this dinosaur was as long as three bendy buses end to end, this tree is twice as high as Nelson's Column) then always check the calculation back the other ways to make sure you haven't missed or inserted a nought. For sure if you do, there will be plenty of people out there ready to check your calculations, and write funny letters.

DON'T MAKE DAFT CALCULATIONS

Let's say there is one case of rabies in Britain in 2005, and then two the following year. To say this is a 100 per cent increase is accurate, but it is still silly.

BEWARE A COMMON PERCENTAGE ERROR

If there were 50 children in a school receiving free school meals last year, and 75 this year, that is an increase of 50 per cent (the difference, 25, expressed as a percentage of the base figure, 50). But if there were 75 last year and 50 this year, that is a decrease of 33 per cent (25 expressed as a percentage of the base figure, which this time is 75). There is a temptation to express the percentage of the lower figure. But you must always express a change based on the original figure.

AVERAGES

Take care whether you have a mean or a median. Imagine a scenario where a firm employs eight people. The managing director earns £100,000 a year. His two assistants earn £75,000 a year. The five other people who work there earn £10,000 a year. There is a pay dispute. The managing director says that the average salary is a respectable £37,500. One of the staff says the average salary is a paltry £10,000. They are both right. The boss is taking the *mean*, the average salary, by adding all the salaries together and dividing by eight. The staff member has taken the salary of the average worker, by calculating the *median*. She has put the numbers in order, and found the middle one.

BE SCEPTICAL

Think carefully where your information comes from. Is it from a government statistical office? Then it is almost certainly correct. Is it from a politician? It might be correct, but a bit spun. Is it from a small, under-funded pressure group? It might simply be wrong, so have a good look at the figures, and try to check them with another source.

Be especially careful about little surveys, especially those conducted by pressure groups with a particular axe to grind. They may have done the survey through their website, so they have in effect polled people who already sympathize with them. This kind of group is self-selecting, and therefore the poll is not representative. If this is the case, there might still be a story, but you should point out how the survey was conducted. Were people invited to return a form, and if so, how many actually did so? Were people asked to fill in something online, in which case maybe what you have got is a survey not of the population as a whole, but of geeky teenage boys.

Some papers make a point, when reporting the results of a poll, in putting at the end of the story when it was carried out, and how big the sample was. This means the readers can make up their own minds about the value of the data.

LINKING RANDOM UNRELATED POINTS

Be very wary of linking bits of information that are not related, implying that one has caused the other. Some Sunday papers are full of stuff like:

Children who bathe less frequently are healthier.

The story goes on to quote from a piece of research, which may be a rather thin piece of research in the first place. It may be, for example, that parents who don't insist on a daily bath may also be the kind of people who do not trot off to the doctor with the children quite so often. The two points may not be related to each other, but to some other, perhaps undocumented point.

A dreadful example of flawed research was a widely reported 1990 study of outcomes of people with cancer who did or did not visit the Bristol

Cancer Help Centre, which pioneered alternative therapies. The research suggested that there was a higher mortality rate for those who had attended the Bristol centre than for those who had received only orthodox treatment. The news caused huge problems for the centre, with cancellations and staff lay-offs. Some years later it was revealed that the sample was skewed, because those going to the Bristol centre had more advanced cancers than the control group.

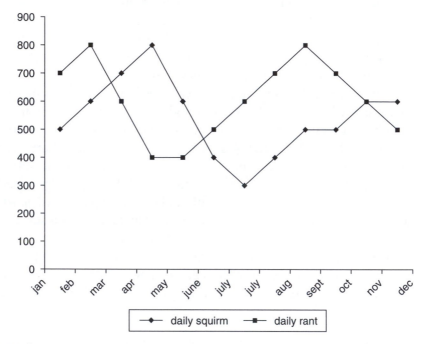

Figure 4

A COMMON FIDDLE

Have a look at Figure 4 above. It shows the circulation figures of two imaginary papers, the figures on the left side being the circulation in 1,000s with the months across the bottom. When the new figures come out, the *Daily Squirm* says its circulation has doubled, and it has overtaken the *Daily Rant,* which is slipping fast. The *Daily Rant* says the *Squirm*'s circulation has crashed, while its own has risen.

These two assertions look contradictory. The *Squirm* has taken its figures from July to December, when it did indeed rise from 300,000 to 600,000, and it has used the figures for the *Rant*'s circulation from September to December. Meanwhile the *Rant* has decided to compare its circulation in December with its figure for May, and so it too can claim a rise. Its claim that the *Squirm* has fallen is also true when the latest figure is compared with the figure for May. For an accurate reflection of what is happening, you must make sure you are comparing like with like, and the longer the view you can take, the more accurate it will be. In both cases looking at the circulation figures compared to a year ago would be more valid.

Politicians used to go in for quite a bit of this sort of thing, especially during elections. In the days when inflation was rampant, the government of the day might make some small change which would affect the retail price index, or the unemployment figures, so that there seemed to be a radical improvement to the figures just before an election was due. Either the reporters have become more sophisticated or the spin doctors cleverer at hiding it, but it seems to me that there is not so much blatant use of dubious figures now as there used to be.

USEFUL WEB ADDRESSES

- **http://lachie.net/maths**   makes all sorts of valuable calculations and conversions for you, including percentages of things, and percentage differences between two numbers. Take care though, because it won't help if you put the wrong numbers in in the first place, and be sure you are getting the percentage of the right thing – see the point above.
- **http://www.xe.com/ucc/** converts currencies.

THE LANGUAGE OF NEWS 1: CHOOSING THE RIGHT WORDS

Choosing the right word is central to success in any kind of writing, and is probably the most complicated subject to work on with student journalists. It is essential to avoid wordiness (see next chapter) but the more pedestrian the language is, the more boring the story is. It is hard to strike the right balance between the direct language of speech, while keeping enough interesting words to make the story lively.

Geoff Roberts, my sixth form English teacher, was fond of this example from Keats's poem *The Eve of St Agnes*:

> Full on this casement shone the wintry moon,
> And threw warm gules on Madeline's fair breast,
> As down she knelt for heaven's grace and boon;
> Rose-bloom fell on her hands, together prest
> And on her silver cross soft amethyst,
> And on her hair a glory, like a saint ...

He liked to paraphrase:

> As Mary knelt to pray, the cold moon
> coming through the stained-glass window
> Made red patches on her white chest,
> pink on her hands, mauve on her cross
> And bright yellow on her hair.

How dull and uninspiring the paraphrase is.

Keats was doing exactly what a good journalist does: including listen-to-me words. Those are ones that Geoff used to say make the hairs on the back of the neck stand up: casement, wintry, gules (which means drops), breast, rose-bloom, amethyst, glory, saint.

The secret of writing news well is to have just enough of these words to make the reader sit up and listen, but not so many as to make the story indigestible. If Keats's poem was a news story it would be indigestible, but a poem is a much more leisured piece of writing, where the effects of the words and images are central, and conveying information is secondary. Keats wouldn't have lasted five minutes as a reporter on the *Sun,* but the principle about attention-grabbing words is the same.

Inexperienced writers often think that slapping on some adjectives and adverbs will enliven a story. Adjectives and adverbs are descriptive parts of speech, and they are rather like icing and marzipan on a cake – if the cake underneath is boring, not only will they not make it any better, they will actually make it worse: the contrast with the topping will make the cake seem even duller. It is the same with descriptive words in a news story. It is interesting that many of the richest and most interesting words in Keats's poem (casement, gules, breast, rose-bloom, glory) are nouns. He has achieved much of the effect through nouns, not adjectives and adverbs.

Colourful lively writing is hard to achieve, and very hard to agree on. One reader may think a piece of writing is brilliant, and another will think it is overdone and too flowery. You have to develop your own style, and hope that your news editor likes it and that the **chief sub** gives you enough space for it.

There was a story about the late John Thicknesse, who was cricket correspondent for the *Evening Standard.* He was much taken by the setting of one of the West Indies cricket grounds and wrote about it at some length and in flowery terms in his report, paid for in those days by the cable word. The sports editor, alarmed at the cost, cabled back 'forget scenery', to which Thicknesse replied 'scenery unforgettable'.

One of my colleagues used to make students write **colour stories** without any adjectives: this forced them to choose their nouns and verbs carefully, so that at least some of them are listen-to-me words. Take this sentence:

The man ran down the road towards the house.

'The man' as a description is very nearly the lowest common denominator, by which I mean it carries almost the smallest amount of meaning possible. The only word lower is 'person', which means even less. If you find yourself writing the word 'man', then don't. Any other word has got to be better than this: lawyer, grandfather, prince, drug-dealer, actor, shopper. The same applies to the word 'people': good news stories almost never use the word 'people', because there is nearly always an alternative: residents, voters, clubbers or students.

Similarly, 'ran' is the lowest common denominator word to describe that movement. What about dashed, swerved, sprinted, darted? And if it was his own home he was running towards as he was being chased, it could be 'safety of his home' rather than 'house'.

The student sprinted down the road towards the safety of his home

describes the same event, but tells us so much more, and is so much more arresting.

There is a theory in the science of linguistics that the less often a word is used, the more meaning it carries. So 'ran' is a very common word, much more common than 'sprinted', and it is easy to see that 'sprinted' carries more meaning: it simply tells us more about what happened. The word shoe carries far less meaning that brogue, trainer, flip-flop, stiletto, pump or the outdated winklepicker. Any of these words would tell your readers a great deal more about the wearer than the word shoe. Trade names carry a lot of meaning, especially in terms of fashion, perfume and cars. Manolo has entered the language since *Sex and the City*. The same goes for food, for example. If you write about someone ordering a salad, it doesn't mean all that much. If you write that she ordered rocket, shaved parmesan and balsamic vinegar dressing, it says so much more.

Try to get as many verbs in as possible: more verbs means more things are happening, and the more things that are happening, the more lively your story will be.

SCENARIO 1: THE EAGLE RISES

Look at this story from the *Guardian:*

Eagle landed: *Graft Spee* emblem salvaged

After resting its wings in mud off the Uruguayan coast for more than 60 years, the bronze eagle that once adorned the pride of the Nazi fleet has risen again.

Para 1: Terrific image – and a 'personalization' of the eagle resting its wings in mud. This idea of bringing the eagle to life continues with it 'clutching the wreath'. 'Bronze eagle' is an arresting phrase, as is 'adorned', 'pride', 'Nazi' and 'risen again'. A lot of the listen-to-me words are verbs: resting, adorned, risen again.

The eagle was salvaged last week from the wreck of the *Graf Spee*, the German pocket battleship scuttled after the Battle of the River Plate in December 1939. The 6 ft, half tonne statue, which was designed by Adolf Hitler, clutches a wreath encircling a huge swastika.

Para 2: Plenty more listen-to-me words: salvaged, wreck, battleship scuttled, clutches, huge, swastika and of course Adolf Hitler. Again note the number of verbs.

Mensun Bound, the British marine archaeologist leading the salvage team, said it was probably the only surviving example of its kind. 'When it came up and I saw the swastika, I knew I was looking at the absolute heart of darkness' he said. 'All the hairs on the back of my neck stood up. It felt like the breath of Hitler himself.'

Paras 3–4: Features a truly excellent quote, focusing on the moment the statue came out of the water, with a vivid description the scene and how the team felt. Note the listen-to-me words in the quote, especially 'heart of darkness' and 'the breath of Hitler himself'.

'When artefacts come out of the water, there is normally lots of cheering and backslapping. But when this Nazi symbol surfaced, there was just silence,' he added.

The *Graf Spee* sank so many Allied merchant ships in the south Atlantic that Winston Churchill sent a fleet to destroy it. After a skirmish with the Royal Navy, it sought repairs in Montevideo and after political wrangling left the port to be scuttled by its captain.

Paras 5–6: The story finishes with essential background about how the ship came to be lying where it was, and how the statue came to be salvaged. These last two paragraphs convey a great deal of information in a very few words, but there are enough listen-to-me words to keep the story lively: Winston Churchill, skirmish, wrangling.

The wreck lay in waters only 30 ft deep until a joint salvage project was launched by private investors and the Uruguayan government two years ago. Its eagle, which is to be sold at auction, has already attracted bids of £15m.

Here is a version with all the interesting listen-to-me words and quotes removed. Notice how the addition of a few words can make a dull story into an arresting one, or vice versa.

A bronze statue from a German battleship which sank off the Uruguayan coast more than 60 years ago has been raised.

The statue of an eagle, wreath and swastika is 6 ft high and weighs half a tonne.

It was salvaged last week from the wreck of the *Graf Spee*, the German battleship scuttled after the Battle of the River Plate in December 1939. The statue was designed by Adolf Hitler.

Mensun Bound, the British marine archaeologist leading the salvage team, said it was probably the only example of its kind. He said it was a very eerie moment when the statue was raised, and the team stood in silence.

The *Graf Spee* sank so many Allied merchant ships in the south Atlantic that Britain sent Royal Navy ships to engage it. The German ship was damaged in the encounter, and put into Montevideo but after a political argument left port and was sunk by its captain.

The ship lay in waters only 30 ft deep until a joint salvage project was launched by private investors and the Uruguayan government two years ago. The statue, which is to be sold at auction, has already attracted bids of £15m.

SCENARIO 2: PANDA DIPLOMACY

The next example is a very different piece from the *Financial Times*. It is an extremely good story, which includes conflict, because there is a diplomatic row brewing. It includes giant pandas, the Beckhams of the animal kingdom. Almost everyone is fascinated by giant pandas for lots of reasons, their cuddliness, looks, rarity, lack of sex drive, and the way they keep their new cubs in their armpits. The FT had a terrific photo of the pair on the front, looking very playful. Of course we don't expect the FT to go overboard with colour writing, but there is just the right amount of listen-to-me words to make the story very readable.

Taipei fury at China's 'disrespectful' panda offer

China's 'panda diplomacy' threatened to backfire yesterday after its offer of two pandas to Taiwan provoked outrage in the island's government.

Para 1: 'Panda diplomacy', which has been used before, is a great phrase, because the two words are so incongruous. They create a tension in the intro which sums up the tension of the whole story: it is odd to use pandas to score diplomatic points. Threatened, backfire, provoked and outrage are good listen-to-me words.

Officials in Taipei accused Beijing of 'disrespect' and 'pro-unification political warfare' after it announced it would give Taiwan a pair of pandas.

Para 2: *Accused, disrespect, warfare are all good lively words.*

The pair, chosen from a pool of 23 candidates, were selected for their cuteness, character and compatibility after a series of genetic tests and 'trial marriages', Beijing officials said.

Para 3: *Candidates is an excellent word, creating a tension by linking the pandas to a word normally used to describe politicians or students taking exams. Cuteness and trial marriage are also listen-to-me words.*

But while the Chinese and Taiwanese media indulged in an orgy of coverage, with revelations of the pandas' favourite foods, hobbies and star signs, Taipei reacted with anger.

Para 4: *Indulged, orgy, revelations, hobbies, anger, all carry a lot of meaning. Words which humanise the pandas add to the humour of the story.*

Joseph Wu, chairman of the Mainland Affairs Council, Taiwan's cabinet-level China policy body, attacked the mainland propaganda as political warfare.

Para 5: *Propaganda and political warfare both keep the story alive and indicate the extent of the political row.*

'They unilaterally announce the pandas will be sent over here in June, without having discussed the latter with Taiwan's government ... that is very disrespectful,' Mr Wu said.

Para 6: *The quote is a good one, taking the story forward by making it clear that it was a unilateral announcement from Beijing, and sourcing Taipei's reaction.*

For a year, Beijing has played down its threat to use force to back its claim to sovereignty over Taiwan, instead launching policy initiatives intended to appeal to Taiwanese opinion.

Para 7: *Threat and force are again both listen-to-me words.*

Such moves are usually double-edged. The proffered pandas, for example, support China's claim to sovereignty over Taiwan, since Beijing no longer gives the endangered animals to foreign countries.

Para 8: *Double-edged is a good word, as is endangered.*

However, many Taiwanese are charmed by the cuddly creatures and opposition parties that support reunification with China have attacked the government as obstructionist.

Para 9: Cuddly is an excellent word. It is not that rare in tabloid papers, but doesn't appear often in the FT, and there is also the alliteration with creatures.

Lien Chan, the former head of the opposition Kuomintang, said yesterday the pandas should not be viewed through the prism of Taiwanese political party colours. 'With pandas, there is no blue and green [the colours of Taiwan's two main parties], only black and white, right and wrong.' Mr Lien said. 'We hope the government will stop politicising this issue.'

Para 10: Excellent quote here, with the politician producing an extended image about the colours of the political parties and the black and white of the pandas.

However, some Chinese internet users blamed Beijing for dragging the lovable *Ailuropoda melanoleuca* into politics.

'Giant pandas should be allowed to live in their own habitat. I oppose this kind of political manoeuvring. Poor pandas,' wrote one poster to a discussion board on the popular portal Sina.com.

In the version below, all the listen-to-me words have been removed, leading to a much less colourful, duller piece which does not engage the reader nearly as much.

> Officials in Taiwan are angry about an offer of two pandas from mainland China.
> They accused Beijing of disrespect and of using the panda offer to seek reunification.
> The two pandas have been chosen for their compatibility after genetic testing and observing them together.
> The media in both China and Taiwan have covered the story of the offer in great detail, but the government in Taipei reacted with anger.

Joseph Wu, chairman of the Mainland Affairs Council, Taiwan's cabinet-level China policy body, attacked the mainland propaganda as political warfare.

'They unilaterally announce the pandas will be sent over here in June, without having discussed the latter with Taiwan's government ... that is very disrespectful,' Mr Wu said.

For a year, Beijing has played down its threat to use force to back its claim to sovereignty over Taiwan, instead launching policy initiatives intended to appeal to Taiwanese opinion. But the offer supports China's claim to sovereignty over Taiwan, since Beijing no longer gives the endangered animals to foreign countries.

However, many Taiwanese are charmed by the pandas, and opposition parties that support reunification with China have attacked the government as obstructionist.

Lien Chan, the former head of the opposition Kuomintang, said yesterday the pandas should not be turned into a political issue.

However, some Chinese internet users blamed Beijing for dragging the pandas into politics.

'Giant pandas should be allowed to live in their own habitat. I oppose this kind of political manoeuvring. Poor pandas' wrote one poster to a discussion board on the popular portal Sina.com.

There are examples in all the tabloids every day showing how a very few colourful and telling words can enliven a story. These examples from the *News of the World* are not the liveliest in terms of content, but this shows how the right choice of words can make a very sharp story:

Education Secretary Ruth Kelly has been forced to make big changes to her schools shake-up to head off a Labour backbench rebellion.

This is only 22 words, it is clear, tells us exactly what has happened, and has plenty of listen-to-me words: forced, shake-up, head off, rebellion. Note the alliteration of 'schools' and 'shakeup' and an internal one with 'backbench' and 'rebellion'.

Detectives hunting the ruthless robbers behind the £50m Securitas heist believe THIS could be the face of the gang's leader.

Only a few words (20), but 'hunting', 'ruthless robbers' (alliteration), 'heist' and 'gang' keep it lively.

Terrorists can marry their way into Britain in a deadly brides-for-rent racket run by a Muslim mullah, the *News of the World* can reveal.

Again, short, to the point, and every word is telling.

These examples are not plastered with extraneous adjectives. They are bright and readable because there are very few words, and very few listen-to-me words, but each one adds so much to the story.

JOURNALISTIC CLICHÉS: OVERDOING THE LISTEN-TO-ME WORDS

The more you read, the more words you will have in your vocabulary, and the bigger choice you will have when it comes to writing. Read lots of newspapers and magazines of course, but try to find time, when there is a story that interests you, to look at several versions on the internet, and see how different papers and websites treat it. But beware, as you strive to give colour to your writing, of overdoing it. Note how the *News of the World* stories above are not full of dramatic words and phrases, they have just enough to make the story lively, without being overwritten.

And beware of following the crowd by using new vogue words which might have seemed interesting and clever a year ago but have turned into journalistic clichés by now. All those who see a lot of journalistic writing, but especially careful sub-editors and journalism tutors, have their own lists of *bêtes noires*.

Recent vogue words have included 'charisma', 'chutzpah' and 'macho'. There was a time when you could hardly find a feature in a newspaper or magazine which didn't have one of these. Fortunately these words are now being used as often or as little as they deserve. Another was 'eponymous': no piece about *Hamlet*, or dozens of other plays or films, was safe from the phrase 'the eponymous hero'. That too has faded slightly – and deservedly so, because the word adds absolutely nothing in terms of meaning or interest.

Current vogue ones are 'dystopia', which almost but not entirely means the opposite of utopia. It means a society such as is depicted in George Orwell's *1984*. The word is not in my Oxford dictionary, although apparently John Stuart Mill used it in the 19th century. Others which are becoming overused are 'zeitgeist', which pops up all over the place, meaning the spirit of a particularly society, and 'edgy', presumably meaning something challenging, or almost unacceptable.

'*** is the new ****' as in 'knitting is the new clubbing', and so on, has been so overused that *Private Eye* has started a very funny column, entitled The Neophiliacs. Other irritating phrases which are around now are 'go figure' used after some facts about something, and 'What's not to like about ****?' 'Ahead of the curve' is another which sounded quite interesting a couple of years ago, but is becoming overused now.

There was a vogue, around the time of the TV serialization of *Pride and Prejudice* for starting features with 'It is a truth universally acknowledged that…' and this was used for all sorts of random assertions about tulips or poor quality housing in Liverpool. No doubt, if there is another version of *Anna Karenina* on the telly we will see a rash of pieces starting 'All happy families are alike...' *The Killing Fields* became another very overused phrase.

One that irritates many people, not just me, is the concept of all sorts of inanimate places or objects being able to see things, as in

The Arsenal ground, which last week saw a magnificent victory ...

The daftest example of this I have ever seen was a story about a TV programme,

... which saw its viewing figures rise from ...

It certainly would be unusual for the programme to be seeing its viewers, rather than the other way round.

Another one is the term 'hosting', and 'being home to'. It is just about okay for a hotel to host something, since at least that is what hoteliers do, but for a university to be home to new courses, as I have read, or an office building to host several suites, is daft. The point about these constructions is that no one ever uses them in speech. No one would ever say:

I have just been at the Arsenal ground, which saw a very poor game ...

Another overused construction, which has sadly been around for a long time, and which seems to be on the increase, is the use of a peculiar future past arrangement when talking about events some time in the past:

It was at Wellingborough that Smith met Joan Sharpe, the woman who was to become his wife.

Or, perhaps even worse:

It was at Wellingborough that Smith met Joan Sharpe, the woman who would become his wife.

This is a favourite of obituary writers, who seem to think that this construction makes the situation more real. But it is just unnecessary. The 'it was at' construction is also unnecessary, though slightly less irritating. What is wrong with:

At Wellingborough Smith met Joan Sharpe, who became his wife.

Another journalistic oddity is 'ahead of', as in:

Union leaders were meeting the chief executive ahead of the board meeting ...

I am baffled as to why anyone would want to use this instead of 'before', which is shorter and more direct. I can't picture anyone saying to a friend:

> I am just going down to the bank ahead of going shopping …

Yet another journalistic cliché is the phrase 'are/is set to'. If you look at stories where this phrase appears, they are sometimes a bit woolly:

> Broxbourne Council is set to ban smoking in pubs after a poll …

This might mean the council really is going to do it, but it might mean that the reporter thinks the council is probably going to do so, but is not absolutely certain. Either way, it is yet another of those expressions which appear in news writing and simply are not used by the rest of the population.

So watch out for vogue words: it is nice to use them when they come into fashion, but try to be the first to stop using them before they get tired and old.

10

THE LANGUAGE OF NEWS 2: SENTENCE STRUCTURE, BREVITY, CLARITY

The 17th century French mathematician and philosopher Blaise Pascal wrote: 'I have made this letter longer than usual, only because I have not had the time to make it shorter.' This remark, which has been attributed to several other people, neatly sums up the difficulty of concise writing. It takes much longer to make a piece of writing as clear and precise as possible; it is far quicker to produce something wordy and waffly. Many non-journalists believe that it is easier to write for the *Sun* or the *Mirror* than for a broadsheet or former broadsheet. The reverse is probably true. Getting a story down to very few words, yet keeping all the action, drama, colour and human interest takes a lot of practice. This is generally known among journalism teachers as word economy.

The best news stories tell your readers as much as possible as briefly as possible. They also do so in language that is easily understood. This doesn't mean news has to be written as in a primary school reader, but just that it must be direct and snappy. A good news story would never contain a sentence which the reader had to look at twice to understand.

It can be very difficult for young journalists to learn the art of simple direct writing. Without wishing to be too critical of humanities teaching at universities, I think that lecturers sometimes do not mind essays being written in an unnecessarily complicated style. They don't always want or expect a literature or history essay to be couched in the most direct language. And they don't penalize students for being wordy. Sometimes, perish the thought, students deliberately waffle around to get to the required word length. Again, this waffle is not always criticized. So it can be hard for humanities graduates wanting to go into journalism to get into the habit of saying something in the simplest way possible.

I spend a lot of time telling students to write in the way that they would speak when standing in the pub talking to friends. This is to help them to avoid the worst kinds of wordiness. I have sometimes used as a news exercise a council document about a proposal to ban parking in an Islington street to allow better access for 'fire brigade emergency vehicles'. Often this phrase then appears in their stories. I suggest they picture themselves standing in the pub when a big red engine goes by with sirens blaring. Would they say: 'There goes a fire brigade emergency vehicle'?

There is no simple formula to help young journalists with word economy, and it can take several years to master concise writing. One way to help would be to read well-written newspapers regularly, especially the tabloids. Study the website of the Plain English Campaign, www.plainenglish.co.uk. This is a pressure group which seeks to make official writing easier to understand. It produces very useful material with advice for clear writing, some of which can be downloaded free. It also makes awards for clarity in official documents and golden bull awards for the worst examples of gobbledegook, and a foot-in-mouth award for the most baffling remark. The whole site makes interesting reading.

If you are working as a journalist, compare the versions of the stories you submit with what appears in the paper. The chances are that a sub will have made them more concise without losing any of the important points.

USE THE SHORTEST FORM OF THE VERB

Work out what is happening, and make sure you use one verb to express that. Avoid this construction, which is known as the present perfect, although it is not in the present:

Leonora has promised to look into the …

If you see the word 'has' or 'have' as part of a verb, ask yourself whether you really need it. These are the most frequently seen unnecessary extra parts of verbs.

Leonora promised to look into the …

is more direct, more punchy and saves space.

AVOID UNNECESSARY EXTRA VERBS

Making plans, reaching agreements, agreeing to accept, deciding to agree, all these and many more are examples of how sometimes two verbs are used when one will do:

John has made plans to travel to…

is far better as

> John plans to travel to …

While

> Jane suffered a broken arm …

can simply be

> Jane broke her arm …

WATCH OUT FOR WORDS WHICH DON'T MEAN ANYTHING

The most common of these is 'currently', which you almost never need. If something is in the present tense, it follows that it is going on currently. If for some reason you have to stress when it is happening, 'now' is shorter and more direct.

> John is currently studying piano at …

does not need the word currently.

Other adverbs/words that are massively overused in both written and spoken English are 'actually', 'really', 'basically' and 'in fact'. Often in spoken English these are used in an attempt to emphasize the sincerity of the speaker. Before writing any of these words consider whether they are necessary: what do they add to the meaning of the sentence? If the answer is 'nothing' then avoid them.

The world 'that' is often unnecessary: the general rule is that if the subject of the first part of the sentence is the same as the subject of the clause introduced by 'that', then the word can be left out.

> Vidhi said that she would come on Thursday

is fine as

> Vidhi said she would come on Thursday.

Don't leave out 'on' in the sentence though; that is still regarded as an Americanism. Similarly,

> Flying to the island of Corfu …

does not need 'the island of ….' You would need this phrase only if there was likely to be doubt in most of your readers' minds about whether it was an island.

> He was treated for shock and subsequently discharged from hospital

does not need 'subsequently'. He could hardly have been discharged before the treatment. Similarly, 'then' is often stuck in when it is perfectly obvious that one event followed another.

WATCH OUT FOR GENERIC WORDS THAT MAKE THINGS SHORTER

> Consultants, house doctors and nurses at St Bartholomew's …

should be

> 'medical staff'.

> Air hostesses and stewards were issued with smoke hoods …

should be

> 'cabin-crew'.

CHOOSE ANGLO-SAXON WORDS RATHER THAN LATINATE ONES

> Building is better than construction
> Begin is better than commence
> Help is better than assist or assistance

USE VERBS INSTEAD OF ABSTRACT NOUNS

Abstract nouns often refer to an action but make it static by using the name of the action, rather than telling us about someone actually performing it. So removing abstract nouns does two useful things: it makes your writing more concise, but it also makes it more active and dramatic. The more verbs, the more things are happening.

> The committee reached a decision …

should be

> The committee decided …

Similarly

> Women with aspirations to reach the top …

should be

Women who want to reach the top ...

This second example does two things, replaces the abstract noun with a verb, and replaces a long Latinate word with a short Anglo-Saxon one.

TELL US ABOUT PEOPLE DOING THINGS, NOT ABSTRACT IDEAS

Always have a picture in your mind of what is going on, what you are actually telling us about. This will help to keep your writing direct and lively.

Public transport usage is expected to increase significantly

could simply be

More people will go on buses.

BEWARE OF LENGTHY SUBSTITUTE WORDS FOR SAID

The more common a word is, the less it matters about repeating it. A word like 'said' is so common, especially in news writing, where the basis of the story is often that someone said something, that you can safely repeat it, possibly even several times in one story. The fact is that readers skim news stories so quickly, looking for the lively points of interest, that the repetition of 'said' goes unnoticed. It is far better than sticking in 'explained', 'asserted', 'commented', which all look rather naff.

BEWARE POLICE/COUNCIL/HEALTH OFFICIALS' JARGON

Jargon is becoming misused to mean slang, but it originally referred to the specialized phrases and words associated with certain occupations.
    There are good reasons why a police officer might say in court:

As I was proceeding in a westerly direction along the Marylebone Road I had occasion to stop the accused ...

All that can be rendered simply in a newspaper as:

> PC James Browne said he stopped Compton in the Marylebone Road.

GIVE US THE ANSWERS NOT THE QUESTIONS

Take care not to be repetitive by telling us the question as well as the answer. So avoid a construction such as:

> Asked whether he would protest to the council, Julian Poynter said: 'I shall certainly take this protest to the council.'

This can almost always be avoided. Of course, it is partly to do with the way you ask questions in the interview. Get into the habit of asking open questions such as 'What will you do now?' so that you get a full answer which can be used as a quote. If you ask 'Are you going to protest to the council?' and Julian replies 'Yes' then you are still a bit stuck for a good quote.

USE CONCISE, EVERYDAY WORDS AND PHRASES

Many of the phrases that follow are taken from council documents, where it is common to find two or three words when one would do. It is worth reading these through many times, and eventually, if you see the phrase 'in an attempt to' you will automatically substitute 'trying to', and so on.

Don't use	Use
acquire	get
in addition to	as well as
additional funding	more money
admitted to	admitted
in advance of	before
an address in Thornhill Square	Thornhill Square
ahead of	before
air hostesses and stewards	cabin crew
approximately	about
asserted that`	said
aspirations	aims/goals
assist	help
in an attempt to	trying to
attempted emergency resuscitation	tried to revive
basis (e.g. on a daily basis)	(OMIT)

budgetary allocation	money, spending
was the cause of	caused
there is a clear financial advantage	it will be cheaper
companies in the private sector	private firms
conduct a poll of	poll
give consideration to	consider
construction	building (sometimes)
was a contributing factor in	contributed to
consultant forensic pathologist	pathologist
council house residents	council tenants
currently	now (or OMIT)
deceased	dead man/woman (deceased is not a lay person's word)
Department of the Environment	often, for local paper, simply the government
in the direction of	towards
domestic premises	homes
due to the fact that	because
economically disadvantaged groups	poor (take care – may not be PC)
establishment	firm, unit, plant
everyone on the electoral roll	voters
exacerbate	worsen
expenditure	spending, cost
exterior	outside
following the airline's agreement	after the airline agreed
for six nights of the week	six nights a week
forensic medical officer	police doctor/surgeon
granted bail	bailed
have an impact on	affect
head up	head
hold consultations with	consult, talk to
hold talks with	talk to
the hours of	(OMIT)
implement	carry out
industry	trade (sometimes) e.g. building trade
inform	tell
make the information known to	tell
initiative	plan
intoxicating liquor	alcohol
legislation	law (or if not passed, bill)
local authority	council

location	place, venue
in the London Borough of Islington	in Islington
meet with	meet (meet with is an unnecessary Americanism)
negative traffic effects	traffic jam, worse traffic
in order to	to
on a daily basis	every day
pedestrian traffic	pedestrians, walkers
the possession of illegal substances	possessing drugs/explosives
the purchase of	buying
at the present time	at present, now
at a price of	costing
prior experience	experience
prior to the submission of	before submitting
private sector institutions	private firms/companies
prohibited	banned
reached a decision	decided
reached an agreement	agreed
refuse collectors on strike action	striking binmen (not PC of course!)
in a relatively short timescale	soon
residence	home
resulted in the death of	killed
as a result of the inhalation of fumes	from inhaling fumes
retail based development	shops
retail outlets	shops
sent to jail	jailed
sentenced to life imprisonment	jailed for life
are set to cost	will cost
subsequently	(very boring word, can almost always be omitted)
substantial proportion of	most, many (meaningless really)
to successfully conceive	conceive (how could you conceive unsuccessfully?)
sufficient capital	enough money
sustained a broken arm	X's arm was broken
suffered a broken arm	(ditto)
take into custody	arrest
together with	with
unauthorized occupiers	squatters
zero cost implications	won't cost anything, will be free

11

THE LANGUAGE OF NEWS 3: GRAMMAR, SPELLING AND PUNCTUATION

ALMOST NO RULES, REALLY

Languages are in a constant state of change, with usages and elements of style which would have seemed wrong at one time becoming acceptable years later, and vice versa. In Jane Austen's novels you can read 'He don't …' which would be considered incorrect today. The list of expressions that would have been incorrect then but are now acceptable is endless.

I am in a shrinking minority who believe, for example, that 'I am going to try and get to the shops' (should be 'try to') and 'alright' (should be 'all right') are not perfect English. These are just a couple of a dozen or so usages which I was taught are wrong, and yet they appear in papers, magazines, brochures and even books. 'Alright' even appears in some dictionaries now, probably rightly, since the dictionary compilers are reflecting usage, not trying to lay down rules.

Amazon tells us 'Your order has dispatched …' which sounds odd to me (what has the order dispatched?) although I am getting used to 'X tested positive' of a sports person, and a 'programme has aired'. All these are active versions of verbs which until recently would have been used as passives: ('He was tested and found to be positive'; 'The programme was aired'). These usages have entered the language, and we have about as much chance of stopping them as the Académie Française has of stopping the tide of Americanisms engulfing their language, like *le brushing, le jogging* and hundreds of others.

There is no doubt that these changes in grammatical rules are happening more and more quickly because of the internet, where so much material out there is written in a colloquial style like that of speech, rather than in a formal 'written' style. In addition, much of this material is either poorly edited or not edited at all. The other agent of change is the lack of attention paid to conventional grammar in schools. With so many citizen journalists around, it seems likely that many of the grammatical rules we adhered to a couple of generations ago will disappear very speedily.

So this chapter will not go at length into the many disputed areas. Lots of grammar books will tell you about when to use 'that' and 'which', about the possessive before a gerund (should it be 'Do you mind Tarquin coming to the pub?' or 'Do you mind Tarquin's coming to the pub?') and so on. Many of these 'rules' are disappearing so fast that I believe it is not worth worrying about them. However, any young journalist or student journalist should spend a great deal of time with the house style book for the publisher/newspaper she is writing for. Maybe the editor, or the chief revise sub, has a bee in her bonnet about split infinitives ('He said he would try to quickly mend the puncture') or the use of a future tense after a past tense: 'He said he will come on Monday' (many people insist on 'He said he would come on Monday'). If some of the points in the style book seem pernickety, well, it isn't worth wasting any energy arguing, or even thinking of arguing. When you become editor you can revise the style book and put in some of the points you feel strongly about.

Beware of the grammar functions of the Word program. It certainly is worth checking why the program has put a green line under something, but many of the Word suggestions need to be rejected. Some are rather esoteric and unnecessary, and others are plain wrong. In addition it simply doesn't pick up some quite serious grammatical errors. So don't think just because your final draft is free of green lines that it is correct.

THE MOST COMMON ERRORS

The main causes of grammatical errors in the work of inexperienced writers almost all come down to the same point: a failure to link one word or phrase correctly to another.

WEAK LINK 1: FAILING TO LINK SUBJECTS AND VERB ENDINGS CORRECTLY

It is very easy to get verb endings right in English. In past tenses the verb is the same whether it is preceded by I, he, we, you or they, as in 'I said, you said, he said'. The same goes for the future tense: 'I will say, you will say' and so on.

Apart from a few irregular verbs, such as To Be, the only time the verb ending changes is in the third person singular present tense, which generally takes an 's'. So 'I say', 'they say', but 'he or she says'. This one point does cause plenty of difficulty. Usually the writer can hear that an s is required, so long as the subject is near enough to the verb. But once there is a phrase in between, things start to go wrong.

> The EU, with the support of trade unions, argues that working long hours are a threat to health and safety.

The first thing to note is that 'argues' is correct, because groups and organizations (apart from sports teams) are almost always singular. The phrase 'with the support of trade unions' is in parenthesis, as evidenced by the commas before and after it, so it is not the subject of the verb 'argues'. But the next verb is wrong, because the subject of 'are' is 'working', a singular idea. The writer has mistakenly used the plural, because the verb follows the plural 'hours'. But 'hours' is not the subject of the verb. It is undeniable that the sentence 'working long hours is a threat' sounds peculiar because of the plural so near the verb. But it is correct. Perhaps a better way round would be:

> ... argues that long working hours are a threat. ...

This sounds better because the word 'hours' then becomes the subject.
  Here is another example of a similar problem:

> Some 187 courses, as well as many a conference and training session, brings in some 3,000 residential guests ...

This is the same mistake the other way round, the singular idea of training session means the writer has put the singular form of the verb (with an 's'), but in fact the plural 'courses' at the beginning of the sentence is the subject of the verb. The long phrase in parenthesis, 'as well as many a conference and training session', has lulled the writer into thinking that 'session' is the subject of the verb immediately after it.
  One way to be sure to get this right is to read your work through out loud quite quickly, so that you get a feel for the whole sentence, and are more likely to link subject and verb correctly. Inexperienced journalists are a bit shy of doing this, but you often see senior people in newsrooms muttering their way through their copy just before submitting it. Another way is to make a point of reading it once through missing out any phrases that could be omitted without changing the meaning. If the writer had read out

> Some 187 courses brings in ...

she would have spotted the error.

WEAK LINK 2: FAILING TO LINK ALL THE VERBS IN A PIECE OF WRITING

The second most common error involving verbs is muddling tenses in a piece of journalism, where for example one eyewitness quote is introduced by 'says' in one sentence but by 'said' in another.

Sometimes a news story can start in the present:

> Residents on the Blackstock Estate are furious about a council plan to ...

and then revert to the past tense:

> Tenants' Association chair Jon Bright said a petition had been drawn up ...

but then you must stick to the past tense for the rest of the story.

Very occasionally in a short, slightly chatty feature piece, especially one based on an interview, you can stick to the present tense, but the main thing is not to muddle tenses.

A specific little error which is quite common is the incorrect linking of a passive verb with a participle. The point about trying to use active verbs whenever possible is discussed in Chapters 3 and 10, but there is no doubt that sometimes a passive form is inevitable, and indeed welcome, to give a slight change of pace. The problem arises when there is a second incomplete verb in the sentence, and the two verbs don't agree correctly:

> The girl was punished by sending her home.

This is a fairly common error. The first verb of the sentence is passive, and it is a good place to use one, since the girl is probably a more interesting Who to start with than the people who did the punishing. But the error comes in the second, subordinate clause, when the present participle 'sending' is active, but has no subject. So the reader tries to link it to the only subject there is, 'the girl', but that doesn't work because she didn't do the sending. The sentence must be recast:

> The girl was punished by being sent home.

WEAK LINK 3: SUBJECTS WHICH END UP WITH PECULIAR UNRELATED VERBS

There is so far as I know no grammatical term for this error, which is quite common in informal writing, and is therefore creeping into what ought to be more carefully constructed work. Here is an example:

A teenage prisoner taken hostage in Bunbury prison last night will increase fears …

This appeared as the intro of a story in a local paper and it is easy to see what is wrong when it is taken out of context. How can this teenager increase fears? It is not the teenager, it is the hostage-taking event that will increase fears. But the reporter, having probably been told plenty of times to go for active verbs and avoid abstract nouns, did not want to make the subject 'hostage-taking' or some such.

What has happened here is that there is a very long phrase making up the subject of the verb: 'A teenage prisoner taken hostage in Bunbury prison last night'. But the subject word is 'prisoner,' and all the rest of the words are adjectival, describing the prisoner. Once you see that, it is easy to understand that the prisoner herself cannot increase fears. The sentence has to be completely recast, something like:

A teenage prisoner was taken hostage and held in a cell for five hours at Bunbury jail last night. Her ordeal will increase fears …

WEAK LINK 4: THE DANGLING MODIFIER

At least this one has a memorable name. Some grammarians call some versions of this a floating or unattached participle. But 'dangling modifier' is such a peculiar phrase, and gives us an odd picture, that perhaps it helps students to remember what this mistake is, and how to avoid it.

After destroying a shuttle, the discovery of the asteroid was likened to the one that killed off the dinosaurs 65 million years ago.

This sentence has a dangling modifier and another oddity, not exactly the same error but a similar one, after it.

It is a good idea to put a participle phrase at the beginning of a sentence from time to time, leaving the main verb until later, to give variety to the writing. But it is essential to link the participle phrase correctly. The phrase at the beginning has a present participle, 'destroying', which needs a subject, and the first one it can connect itself to is 'discovery'. But the discovery did not destroy the shuttle, it was the asteroid. Similarly, there is a missing link in the second half of the sentence. The subject of the main verb 'likened' should be 'asteroid' but again it becomes discovery. The discovery can't be likened to another asteroid.

The sentence can be corrected by simply taking out 'the discovery of', which then removes both errors. The next sentence would have to explain something about the discovery.

The classic example used to illustrate the dangling modifier is:

Running for a bus, the car knocked her over ...

'Running', part of a verb, needs a subject and will automatically link itself to the next main subject which appears. That subject becomes 'car', but it was not the car which was doing the running. The sentence must be recast:

Running for a bus, she was knocked over ...

WEAK LINK 5: THE WANDERING PRONOUN

Pronouns (such as he, she, it, they) are used in place of nouns, as the word suggests. Often errors occur when the writer knows what she means by 'it' or 'they', but the sentence is constructed in such a way that the main noun for which the pronoun is standing in is too far away, or simply not there at all.

This kind of construction appears all the time in spoken language, and the hearers can understand what is meant, but when written down the sentence becomes unsettling because of the missing link.

The museum is now exhibiting an example of a black Caribbean front room and details of how they have changed since mass migration to Britain began after World War II.

The error is fairly clear here – the pronoun should refer to 'front room', but the pronoun is plural and 'room' is singular. Changing 'they' to 'it' doesn't help, because it isn't one room that has changed. There is probably no way to correct this without repeating the word 'room':

The museum is now exhibiting an example of a black Caribbean front room. There are details of how Caribbean front rooms have changed since mass migration to Britain began after World War II.

In these next two examples, the pronouns are genuinely wandering – they have no noun to attach themselves to at all:

In London, for example, homebuyers are also competing against professional landlords and overseas buyers, which increases prices.

'Which' cannot refer back to the whole sentence 'homebuyers are competing ... overseas buyers'. It needs to refer to a noun – which would have to be 'competition between the groups'. But again, the writer had been told to avoid abstract nouns. Probably two sentences are needed:

In London, for example, homebuyers are also competing against professional landlords and overseas buyers. This competition increases prices …

Here is another example which might seem fairly sound:

Huguenots fled to London throughout the 1700s until at its peak they made up 5 per cent of the city's population.

The snag here is 'its peak'. 'It' is a pronoun and needs to refer to a phrase something like 'the Huguenot population' but that phrase simply isn't there. It could be inserted just after 'peak', although then the repetition of 'population' jars, so that needs altering:

Huguenots fled to London throughout the 1700s until at its peak the Huguenot population made up 5 per cent of the city's residents.

A related problem with pronouns is the misuse of the personal pronouns 'I', 'me' and 'myself'. People feel that to use 'I' implies an arrogance, so they think 'me' or 'myself' sounds more restrained. This however does not make it right. If there is a compound subject or object, such as 'Jane and I', or 'the soldiers and me', it is essential to check the sentence with just the personal pronoun, leaving Jane and the soldiers out of it.

He spoke to I

is easily felt to be wrong, so

He spoke to Josanne and I

is wrong as well: it must be

He spoke to Josanne and me.

Similarly,

The rebels waved their guns at the soldiers and myself

is wrong, though sadly increasingly common.

The rebels waved their guns at me

is right, so 'me' is what should be in the longer sentence as well.
    Worse, but common, are the constructions:

Peter and myself will be going to the pub …
Me and Peter will be going to the pub …

If you get rid of Peter, you can see more easily that 'myself' is wrong here; it should be:

Peter and I will be going to the pub ...

WEAK LINK 6: THE RANDOM 'BUT' (OR 'ALTHOUGH', 'HOWEVER', ETC.)

This caption appeared recently below a photo of a Miss World contestant:

Miss Barbados is training to be a lawyer, but is worried about the rainforest.

It still didn't look perfect in the second edition, although it was improved to:

Miss Barbados is training to be a lawyer and is worried about the rainforest.

The first one is a good example of the random 'but'. Words like 'but', 'although', 'however' and the old-fashioned 'notwithstanding' or 'nonetheless' must link two ideas which are in antithesis, which have a tension or negativity between them. So either:

Miss Barbados is training to be a lawyer, but has failed some of the exams.

Or:

Miss Barbados flies across the Atlantic twice a week, but is worried about the rainforest. [referring to the global warming caused by air travel]

Both would be fine.
   The problem is that the two ideas in the first example are not in contrast. The second, where the 'but' was replaced by 'and', is better and not incorrect, but the two totally different ideas still sit a little oddly together in the same sentence. The error arises quite often with inexperienced writers, who want to vary the length of sentences, and find that slapping a 'but' between a couple of ideas makes for an easier construction than arranging complex sentences involving subordinate clauses.

WEAK LINK 8: THE DISJOINTED COMPARISON

There are two problems here. The first is to do with 'as good as', and is rather similar to the pronoun problem. Check it in the same way as with the pronouns: reduce the sentence to its bare bones, make sure it works, and then put the extra bits back in.

> Pratap's story was as good, if not better than, Wayne's.

If you take out the little bit between the commas ('if not better than'), you can see that the world 'as' is missing. It should be:

> Pratap's story was as good as, if not better than, Wayne's.

The second error arises when the second part of the comparison is not correctly related to the first.

> Pratap's story was better than Wayne.

You need to use 'Wayne's' to stand in for 'Wayne's story', otherwise you end up comparing a story to a person.

WEAK LINK 9: THE UGASP

This error is increasingly common, is not seen by some as an error at all, and has become so famous that there was a lengthy correspondence about it in *The Times* a few years ago.

The acronym stands for Ungrammatical Gender Ambiguous Singular Pronoun. What it means is that in these days of political correctness, writers do not want to imply that everyone is male, but they also do not want the clumsy s/he arrangement.

So you find

> The applicant must note on the form whether they will be away from their home address during the coming month.

'They' is a Ugasp. It is ungrammatical, because it is a plural and should not follow the singular 'applicant'. It has been used because it is gender ambiguous, and does not imply that only men or women might apply for the job, and it is technically a singular pronoun, though it is undoubtedly in reality a plural one.

The Ugasp can very often be avoided, and should be avoided if at all possible as it looks ugly and jars the reader.

> A journalist should never reveal their sources

is far better written as

Journalists should never reveal their sources.

In the second version there is no ugly Ugasp, and no political incorrectness.

The Ugasp has become so common that people use it even when they don't need to. So you find:

The applicant does not have to tell us they are pregnant.

Similarly:

You kicked your victim in the testicles and went on to break their nose.

THE WEAKEST LINK OF ALL: ONLY

'Only' is probably the most misplaced word in the language. In speech it is generally easy to tell from the inflections of the voice which idea the word should correctly be linked to. But in writing it is much more important to get it in the right place. Have a look at this sentence:

John played the piano at the party because Jane copied one piece of music.

It is possible to put 'only' in seven different places in this sentence, and each one means something different, although admittedly some are a bit odd.

Only John played the piano at the party because Jane copied one piece of music.

Peter didn't play.

John only played the piano at the party because Jane copied one piece of music.

He didn't tune or polish it.

John played only the piano at the party because Jane copied one piece of music.

He didn't play the saxophone.

John played the piano only at the party because Jane copied one piece of music.

He didn't play in the pub.

John played the piano at the party only because Jane copied one piece of music.

Jane's copying of the music was the reason he played.

John played the piano at the party because only Jane copied one piece of music.

It was important that Jane copied it.

> John played the piano at the party because Jane copied only one piece of music.

It was important that only one piece was copied.

There can be similar pitfalls with 'even', 'still', 'nearly', and 'almost' but 'only' is the one which most often upsets revise editors and other people who care about language. For what it is worth (probably not a lot), if one of these words is in the wrong place, it is technically called a misplaced limiting modifier. Be sure that it is placed immediately before the idea to which it refers.

TWO FINAL COMMON ERRORS

A SENTENCE WITHOUT A VERB

You don't often see this error in publications, but it crops up quite often in students' writing. Every complete sentence, that is, the group of words between two full points, must have a main verb. You can get away without one in the most informal style, perhaps in a first-person column:

> Paul was drunk. Very drunk. Very very drunk.

But it jars the reader in any other slightly more formal style. Look at this example:

> The council decided to put off the decision about the late licence. Because members felt they did not have enough information.

It is a sad fact that the Word program does not put a green line under the above sentence, and yet any experienced sub would say that it is wrong. The second sentence is not complete because it does not have a main verb. It would be complete without 'because', although the two sentences then feel slightly disjointed and staccato. The 'because' needs to link itself to the previous idea, probably with a comma.

There is unfortunately no magic rule to explain this. Perhaps the only way is to read a lot, write a lot, and try to get a feel for when a sentence is incomplete.

DEFINING AND DESCRIBING CLAUSES

A lot is talked about 'that', 'which' and 'who', and older grammar books set out rules for 'that' versus 'which' and their uses to define or describe. Usage is changing pretty rapidly and not many people think the distinction is important. So the way to be sure that you have defined rather than described, or vice versa, is to use commas in the right place.

The man, who was wearing a hat, got off the bus.

The phrase with commas round it can be removed, and the sentence still makes sense. We are talking about one man, and he happened to be wearing a hat. The hat is simply telling us a bit more about him. The phrase about the hat can be removed without altering the meaning. This means it *describes* the man, it doesn't *define* him. If you remove the commas, the clause is not in parenthesis, and therefore cannot be removed:

The man who was wearing a hat got off the bus.

This tells us that there were two or more men involved, but we are particularly considering the man with the hat. Without the commas this clause *defines* the man; it is an essential part of the sentence because it tells us which man we are talking about. From the sense of this sentence we know there were other men on the bus who were not wearing hats.

The point about commas is discussed further on. The idea of taking out phrases or clauses with commas round them helps in lots of ways, partly in this question of defining, but also to help to use the right part of the verb, and to avoid mistakes with 'I', 'me' and 'myself'.

PUNCTUATION

It is essential to get punctuation right, because incorrect punctuation can alter meaning or make it difficult for the reader to grasp a sentence in one glance. Often incorrect punctuation simply irritates the reader, looks sloppy and creates unnecessary work for the subs.

One of my best students, who has always done interesting work and writes in a lively style, did some work experience which involved careful editing. She talked afterwards about being 'institutionalized'. I can see what she meant, and I can see that those interested in ideas, in reportage, in arresting word pictures, might feel that fiddling around with commas and colons is simply too boring. The fact is though that the main punctuation rules are simple, easily grasped, and worth sorting out very early on in your career. It is like washing up. It might not be great fun, but there is simply no point in doing it at all if you don't do it properly. It is better to be pernickety, or – that dreadful word – anal, about these rules early on in your career. Get them learned so that they are second nature, and then you can concentrate on the creative side, safe in the knowledge that you will get the punctuation right unconsciously.

THE FULL POINT

The full point (or full stop) denotes a pause if the writing were being read aloud. Imagine it as three very short beats. There is nothing much to say about it, except that you need to put one at the end of every sentence and paragraph. If you don't bother, someone else will have to put it in, and you will seem slapdash. In Britain headlines do not take full points, or generally any other punctuation, and neither do picture captions unless they are lengthy.

Avoid little rows of dots to show you have missed something out. Students are quite fond of doing this when they haven't got a full quote, or don't want to use it. You almost never see this in professionally produced work.

THE SEMICOLON

The semicolon is a slightly shorter pause, the equivalent of two very short beats. It is not used very often in news writing, but it is useful on occasion. Use it when the two ideas are related, and almost but not quite separate enough to need two sentences:

> Many of the residents near the school are unhappy about the proposed extension; parents too are worried about possible disruption.

A semicolon is also used in a list of items when each item is rather lengthy and already has a comma in it:

> The team consisted of Anna McKane, the course director; Barbara Schofield, the radio tutor; Rosie Waterhouse, the investigative feature writer, ...

Don't confuse the semicolon (dot and comma below), with the colon (two dots).

THE COLON

For journalists the colon has four uses. First, it is used when the second half of the sentence explains the first:

> Many of the residents near the school are unhappy about the proposed extension: they say the building will be too large for the site.

Compare this example with the one above, which uses the semicolon. Here the second half explains the first half. In the example where a semicolon is used, the two ideas are similar, but the second does not explain the first.

Second, the colon is used at the beginning of examples, as above, and to introduce lists. For example:

> The zoo housed a variety of mammals: tigers, wolves, zebras, lions, and giraffes.

Third, it is used specifically in journalism for picture captions, when a phrase is often used after a name:

> Miss Barbados: worried about the rainforest

The most important use for journalists is to introduce quotes. Almost every publication uses this arrangement for quotations, so it is worth learning it as soon as possible.

> Lynette said: 'My family all want Fido back as soon as possible.'

Note this structure, and stick to it: Name, then 'said', then colon, then open quote, then capital letter. And note that with a full sentence in quotes, the point is inside the closing quote mark.

THE COMMA

This is the tiniest of pauses, just one beat. The comma is the one most often wrongly used, and not just in students' work. You see either too many or too few commas all over the place in official documents, brochures and other material. On the whole, it seems that there is a tendency to put in more commas than are needed. So probably the first rule is, if in doubt, leave it out.

The best test is to read the work aloud to yourself, trying to read it in such a way that a first-time listener would understand it. Listen to the sound of your voice and if it goes down slightly on any word, it is probable that you need at least a comma after that word. You might of course need the next grade of punctuation, the semicolon or the full point. When reading through your work, tap very quickly on your knee: three for a full point, two for a semi-colon and one for a comma. This might help to work out whether you have got the punctuation in the right place.

Use commas between items in a list:

> Flopsy, Mopsy, Cottontail and Peter.

but not before the 'and' unless you are writing for a US publication.

Use it between adjectives that are similar:

Be bloody, bold, and resolute.

Shakespeare put a comma before 'and', so who are we to argue? But don't put commas between adjectives if they all say something quite different. This is said to be a cumulative list of adjectives, meaning they all add something to the description:

A big red shiny apple.

Read these two examples out loud. With the Shakespeare one it is easy to hear the voice going down slightly, indicating where the commas need to be. In the phrase about the apple, the voice doesn't go down at all.

Use commas at the beginning and end of bits which could be left out:

She came from Moseley, Birmingham, and went to university in London.
Tony Blair, the prime minister, said ...
Caspar Benedict, a lorry driver, was the first to stop ...

In all these cases the phrase with the commas before and after could be missed out without losing the sense.

There is a growing tendency in journalism to adopt the construction which makes someone's job, family situation or other attribute into a title. Many older journalists dislike this but now it is so widespread that it must be considered acceptable.

Prime minister Tony Blair said ...
Lorry driver Caspar Benedict was the first on the scene ...
Battling grandmother Jenny Wright accused the council ...

and so on. This is one of those peculiar usages which appear only in journalism. You can't imagine someone using this construction in normal speech. It is here to stay, and in spite of bans on it in some broadsheet or ex-broadsheet papers, it is becoming more common.

However, an error is creeping in, where a writer uses the job or attribute as a title, and then sticks some commas in as well. This is wrong. It is either:

The prime minister, Tony Blair, said ...

Or:

Prime minister Tony Blair said ...

If you put the commas in, you must put a 'the' in. If you don't, as the commas mean the second phrase could be left out, you are left with an ungrammatical

> Prime minister said ...

Use a comma to show when a descriptive phrase or clause is defining, rather than describing (see above).

You usually need a comma if you put a subordinate clause or phrase at the beginning of the sentence:

> Because of the rail strike, the family were not able to get home.

In other cases where a comma might be used it is optional. Look at the next couple of sentences after the heading about quotation marks; some people would like commas in the middle of both, but there is no hard and fast rule. Use the reading aloud test and try to hear whether your voice goes down slightly.

QUOTATION MARKS

Study the style book carefully and make sure you stick to the publisher's rules regarding quotation marks (also called inverted commas). Many publications now use single quotes in most cases, but some still use double. If the general rule is for single, then quotes within quotes will have to be double.

> Arif said: 'I lost my way home.'

Note this quote is a complete sentence, so the full point is inside the quote mark.

> Arif said: 'I got to the end of the lane and thought, "wherever am I?"'

Note that a quote within a quote is introduced by a comma. Note also that you must close all the quotes in order.

Inexperienced writers are very fond of sprinkling random little quotes around odd words. Sometimes they think the word they are using is not entirely appropriate, so it will look better with quotes round it. Sometimes they are trying to get a quote from someone, but seem to end up with only one word. A news editor at Reuters put a total ban on what he called broken quotes and since I started teaching I have often wished I had his power. They are best avoided. If there are a lot of them they hold up the flow for the reader, and at worst they just look naff, as if the writer did not have the strength of her convictions.

There are occasions when they are needed, if you want to make absolutely clear that this specific word was used.

> When he was prime minister John Major once referred to some cabinet colleagues as 'bastards'.

It is pretty important to make clear that he used this word. Note that since the quote is not a complete sentence, the full point goes outside.

PARENTHESES: COMMAS, DASHES AND BRACKETS

See above for an explanation of commas used to mark the beginning and end of a phrase or clause which could be left out. Note that you must get a comma at the beginning *and end* of the item in parenthesis.

You can use two dashes instead, and this gives a rather informal feeling to the writing:

> Fiona – what a girl – was at the party.

A single dash used to be regarded as incorrect, but it now appears in lots of journalism. It makes the writing seem quite chatty, and is possibly not appropriate for a serious news story:

> The students went out most evenings – usually to the pub.

Avoid brackets almost entirely. You see them in journalistic writing only in very specific cases. You should use brackets when you need to give a conversion from one currency to another, from metric to imperial measurement, and when you want to use the initials of an organization further down the story. So:

> The dress cost $345 (£200)
> The National Union of Journalists (NUJ)

But don't put the abbreviation in if you are mentioning the organization only once.

And don't produce irrelevant conversions. Distance in Britain is measured in miles, in spite of some efforts by politicians years ago to move to kilometres. So there is no need to translate a distance in Britain into metric. But of course if you are writing about France, and a distance is in kilometres, then you need the conversion to miles in brackets. Make sure your conversion is rounded up or down to roughly the same degree as the original figure. So not:

> The children had walked the 130 km (80.77 miles) from Rouen to their home in Paris.

Clearly the 130 km has been slightly rounded, so the figure for miles must be too. There is an old joke that after Elizabeth Taylor said 'I feel like a million dollars' a story appeared saying:

> Elizabeth Taylor said: 'I feel like a million dollars (£564,815).'

Students are sometimes fond of sprinkling brackets around in a feature, because they can do it in essays, and it is an easy way to explain something without making a sentence too unwieldy. But you almost never see brackets in journalistic writing, other than in the two cases above.

There is a specific use for the square bracket, which shows that you have inserted something into a quote for the sake of clarity. So if your interviewee says:

> 'They were really looking forward to it and were so excited.'

you might need:

> 'They were really looking forward to [the holiday] and were so excited.'

THE HYPHEN

Missing hyphens sometimes don't matter all that much, but occasionally the lack of one can lead to an exotic unintentional meaning:

> Fresh diver caught scallops
> Problems associated with eating disordered children
> 30 odd students

These are all odd thoughts, and then there is the old chestnut:

> extra marital sex

All need hyphens to avoid confusion:

> Fresh diver-caught scallops
> Problems associated with eating-disordered children
> 30-odd students
> extra-marital sex

In three of these cases the hyphen is needed to make sure the two words are linked to each other and then *as an entity* linked to the noun. Without the hyphen both of the two adjectival words (they are not all strictly adjectives) link themselves independently to the final noun. Without the hyphen we end up with 'eating children', 'odd students', and 'extra sex', which is not what the reader means. In the first example, without the hyphen there is a danger we will think of a 'fresh diver', whereas 'fresh' belongs to 'scallops', and 'diver-caught' belong together.

A recent email from Richard Dixon, chief revise editor at *The Times*, highlighted a good one:

STYLE: 'HYPHENS DON'T MATTER', A SEASONAL REFLECTION

We have discovered a rather dangerous item in copy today: an electric red lace-up basque, on sale – not surprisingly, perhaps – at Marks & Sparks. It is probably an electric-red lace-up basque.

Yours, shocked,

Richard

You need to be careful which words must be linked as pairs, before being linked to the main noun.

Two pairs of compound adjectives ought to be the limit. There is a much-quoted one on the internet:

Low cost easy to use web based document management system.

This is indigestible, and could have been rendered as

Cheap and simple web system for managing documents.

Of course, no one selling something would want to describe it as cheap, which has now come to mean of little value as well as of low price.

SPRINKLED CAPITALS

Many writers are too fond of sprinkling capital letters around when they are not needed. Use capitals only for genuine titles of people and organizations, such as the Pope and Islington Council. Capitals should also be used for titles of books or essays, as in *Investigative Journalism*. But in the text itself this phrase would be lower case, and in this country (but not always abroad) headlines which are in lower case take capitals only for names of people or organizations.

In general, you are more likely to be correct if you go through your copy removing capitals and putting almost everything in lower case, unless you're absolutely certain a capital is required.

THE APOSTROPHE

So we come to the final and most horrific grammar problem, which probably leads to the largest number of errors. There are still plenty of us around whose teeth are set on edge by a missing apostrophe, or worse, one put where it is not needed. Searching 'apostrophe' on Google brings up two million results, so there are plenty of people thinking and writing about it.

It really is not that difficult to get right, and yet some of the brightest students have trouble with it. It goes without saying that the grammar function of the Word program can't get it right. I recently received a piece of writing with the phrase

Neil will speak about his father's passionate love for the city and its Cathedral.

The Word program had put a green line under 'its', and suggested 'it's'. It's (*sic*) enough to make you weep.

Part of the difficulty is that nowadays we see so many examples of apostrophes used incorrectly. As every language teacher knows, the way to get things right is to see other people getting them right.

The notorious 'greengrocer's apostrophe' (note the apostrophe, because it is a possession belonging to the greengrocer), which appears on plurals of fruit and veg on market stalls, has been around a long time. But now there are apostrophes on all sorts of other signs, and websites devoted to photos of them. People are particularly fond of putting apostrophes after vowels, after numbers, and after abbreviations. Almost none of these is needed. The only time an apostrophe is needed for a plural is with a lower-case single letter, when without it the sense might be difficult to grasp:

How many s's are there in Mississippi?
Mind your p's and q's.

At any other time, if you feel an apostrophe coming on, think carefully about the word and check whether what you have is a plural. If you do, then don't put an apostrophe.

The only other times when apostrophes are needed are when a letter is missed out, or for a possessive. In fact, the possessive appears to stem from centuries ago when 'his' was used as a possessive:

Shakespeare his theatre

gradually became

Shakespeare's theatre

So possibly the possessive apostrophe also originally denoted something missed out. Compare the following correctly placed apostrophes:

The dog's bone (possessive and one dog so apostrophe before the s)
The dogs were asleep (plural, no apostrophe)
The dogs' bones (possessive and more than one dog, therefore apostrophe after the s)
The 1970s (plural, no apostrophe)
The MPs were revolting (plural, no apostrophe)
The MP's mistress (possessive, one MP, therefore apostrophe before the s)
The MPs' mistress (several of them sharing, so apostrophe after the s)

The only other time you need apostrophes is with contractions such as 'don't'. These do not present much difficulty in formal writing, but they can crop up in more informal writing:

Sharon's coming to the pub.

This is a contraction for 'Sharon is', and therefore an apostrophe is needed.

You're the one I am looking for.

This is a contraction of 'you are', and again that is why there is an apostrophe.

The last problem is 'its' and 'it's'. To distinguish the possessive from the contraction of 'it is', the possessive 'its' does not have an apostrophe.

The dog ate its bone (possessive, no apostrophe)
It's cold outside (contraction of 'it is', therefore apostrophe needed)

APOSTROPHE CHECKLIST

When you have written something, look through it and stop every time you come to noun ending in s.

1   Is the noun a possessive? Then you need an apostrophe, providing the word is not 'its'(see below). If it's a singular noun the apostrophe comes before the s. If the noun is plural, put the apostrophe after the s.

2   Is the word 'its'? Does it stand in for 'it is'? If so, put an apostrophe. If not, don't. As an extra insurance, every time you see 'it's', read it as 'it is'. If it makes sense like that, you have got the apostrophe right. If it doesn't, you haven't.

If you are one of the many who has difficulty with this, make a determined effort to become one of those who doesn't; it really isn't all that hard. Make a few flash cards and get them out at the bus stop. Put a couple of (correct) examples on the fridge door. This doesn't make you institutionalized or anal, it just makes you the kind of person who gets the saucepans clean.

SPELLING

When I mention this word to a group of students, I can almost feel them all thinking: 'I don't need to listen to this bit, the Word program does this for me.' Well, it is true that Word does alert you to misspellings. But it is not the perfect answer for lots of reasons.

Some students were recently writing pieces which mentioned a very famous Booker prize-winning author. The name came out in two students' copy as

Salmon Residue.

The students must have used the spell check function in the way it most definitely should *not* be used. When they had written their pieces they ran a spell check, quickly saying yes to all the corrections which the program offered. Of course it offered Salmon for Salman and Residue for Rushdie, and in their haste to meet a deadline the students simply accepted what was offered without checking every word.

The only satisfactory way to use the spell check is as you go along, as you would use a dictionary if writing in long-hand. Watch for the red line, sort out each one as you go, checking whether you are happy with what you have got, or whether you need to think again about a particular word. The second way it should be used is to pause if you can't spell a word and use the program dictionary to look it up as you write it. That way you will see things spelled correctly all the time. Spelling is learned by recognition: the more you check as you go along, and look at the correct spelling, the easier it will be to remember it.

There are other reasons why the Word program should be used with caution. Many computers have built-in American spellings, and if that is the case, the spell check is likely to make things worse. Second, it won't help you if you have simply got the wrong word. You also need to be wary of the internet. There are lots of helpful internet sites with lists of the most commonly misspelled words, but one which lists 30 most commonly misspelled words sadly gets two of them wrong itself.

Another difficulty is that many email programs do not have a spell checker and although very informal writing has come to be accepted on emails, it would be worth having your emails written grammatically and spelled correctly. You may well need to email prospective employers about yourself, you might need to email feature pitches, or even copy a piece of writing into an email for ease of transmission. There is no substitute for a small dictionary.

The most commonly misspelled word on the internet is apparently 'minuscule'. Fortunately it can't be needed that often in journalistic copy. The variant with two i's is now so common that I guess we can expect to see it in dictionaries of the future. I have restricted myself to a list of ten words, which are both very frequently misspelled, and also likely to be needed in news writing. These are the correct versions:

accommodate
conscious
acquit
embarrass
necessary
separate
consensus
occurrence
harassment
desperate

It is worth learning these carefully, it will save time in the long run.

Then there is the problem of simply using the wrong word. The following pairs are in the order that it seems to me they are most frequently misused:

- **Imply** means to suggest something in the way you say or write it; **infer** is something readers or listeners do when they deduce something. **Infer** is rarely used, so it is far more likely that the word you want is **imply**.

  When he said he did not like the story, he implied we should have made more effort. We inferred from that that he thought we were not working hard enough.

- **Luxuriant** means a thick, full growth of something; **luxurious** means rich or costly.

Her luxuriant hair got very wet in her luxurious bath.

- **Militate** means to fight or argue against something; **mitigate** means to reduce the severity of something.

  In mitigation his lawyer said he had not been in trouble before, but the severity of the attack militates against his early release.

- **Ensure** means to make sure of something, **insure** means to arrange some kind of financial or legal cover against theft, for example.

  I ensure the car will not get wet by putting it in the garage. I insure the car against theft by paying money to an insurance company.

HOMOPHONES

A homophone pair is two words which sound the same, but have two different spellings with two different meanings. Getting an incorrect homophone is probably the second most common type of error after apostrophes.

I used to think that there were only a few pairs of homophones. Since I began to collect them a few years ago, I realize there are scores of them. Some are the very obvious and boring ones like license/licence, their/there and site/cite/sight. But some give rise to lovely images, like the throws of passion, and one I saw in some sports copy described a footballer who was rather full of himself as a pre-Madonna.

The *Guardian*, in its wonderful corrections and clarifications columns, which are so funny that they are regularly collected into books, runs a homophone corner which highlights some good ones. Here is my current homophone list. I am adding to it all the time.

- The centre of a church is an **aisle** but a land mass surrounded by water is an **isle**.
- You sit on a **beach** by the sea, but under a **beech** tree in the woods.
- Santa came down the chimney **bearing** gifts, not realizing he was **baring** all.
- If you break through a line of soldiers, you would create a **breach** (gap). But another name for trousers is **breeches**. A woman who dominates her husband is said to be wearing the breeches.
- He was a **boarder** in the house near the German **border**.
- **Bowl** is a round thing with fruit in it, **bowel** is the last bit of the digestive system.

- The **burghers** of a city (important leaders/business people with money) probably do not eat many **burgers** from McDonalds.
- **Ceased** means ended, **seized** means not working, jammed in some way. Your brakes might **seize**, which would mean they would **cease** working.
- A **censor** decides if a film/play is too rude, or an army censor stops a reporter from releasing information about troop movements, etc. If you **censure** someone, it means strongly criticize. In parliament, a motion of censure against the government is a very serious issue. A **censer** is a casket to distribute the smoke of burning incense.
- The **Czech** man **checked** his bank account before writing the **cheque**.
- Mrs Jones rushed to grab the curtain **cord** while a surprised Mr Jones fell on to the piano, striking the perfect **chord**.
- You pay someone a **compliment** if you admire his shirt. But the shirt **complements** his jeans if it tones with them and adds something to the ensemble.
- People who sit on councils are **councillors**. People who listen to the troubles of others are **counsellors**.
- The council was determined to **curb** the drunken **kerb**-crawling.
- Baby swans are **cygnets**. Some people wear monogrammed **signet** rings.
- If you are trying to calm a situation down, you are trying to **defuse** it (i.e. take the electricity out of it). But something which is **diffuse** is muddled or rambling, or spread out. Diffuse light is the opposite of a beam of torchlight.
- The first **draft** of his article was complete rubbish because he had had too much **draught** beer last night.
- You have an **effect** on someone, if you make them feel/act differently. This is almost always a noun. As a verb, you **affect** (influence) someone with your charm. The exception to this is that you **effect** a change (effect in this rare example is a verb).
- Wallace was no longer **fazed**, it was very clear that Gromit's **phase** of silent protest was going to last for a while.
- Someone who was **formerly** a councillor used to be one. A councillor **formally** proposes a motion.
- In the **foreword** to her book, she explained the way **forward** for feminists.
- Water **fowl** (birds) will not swim in water which is **foul** (smelly).
- He walked with a rolling **gait** towards the **gate** in the wall.
- A type of bear is a **grizzly**. Someone with grey hair might be said to be **grizzled**. But if you find a corpse, it might be **grisly**. If you tried to eat it, it might be **gristly**.
- He tends to **groan** when he realizes his facial hair has **grown**.

- He hung him by the ear to a coat **hanger**, on the southern wall of the aircraft **hangar**.
- I wish the blister on my **heel** would **heal**.
- **Hordes** of vandals attacked the islanders, because they wanted to **steal** their **hoards** of gold, which were not kept safely in **steel** boxes.
- Policemen have to **elicit** the truth from criminals about their **illicit** activities.
- Hannah used her **insight** on the school's working to **incite** a revolution.
- You lean on a wall, and in the past tense you might have leaned or **leant**. But you **lent** someone some money.
- He **led** the way through the maze, carrying his bullets made of **lead**. But the present tense of **led** is **lead**.
- A **leech** is a horrid little black slug thing. But water **leaches** out of a pond or river.
- The sky may be **lightening** (getting less dark) but there is still a possibility of thunder and **lightning**.
- I am **loath** to go to the pub with Gerald because I **loathe** him.
- Your trousers might be **loose** (not tight-fitting) but you are unlikely to **lose** them.
- The lady of the **manor** did not have very good **manners**.
- Eating **mussels** makes your **muscles** stronger.
- Only **one** person **won** the lottery this week.
- He found that the **personnel** department (often now irritatingly called human resources) were too **personal** in their questions (they asked him about his love life).
- My Uncle Mary **passed** away last year. Looking back on the **past** we realized he was a great man who wanted to be a woman.
- You **peddle** something if you sell it. But you **pedal** along on a bike.
- Reading Tolstoy's novel War and **Peace** is a **piece** of cake (not).
- People who are voting go to the **polls**. But a long thin piece of wood is a **pole**.
- You **pour** cream on your strawberries, or **pour** scorn on someone; you **pore** over a document or book (meaning read very carefully); but the cat cleans its **paws**.
- The **principal** of the college accused his secretary of a lack of **principles** when she tried to seduce him (principal means most important, first).
- You **raise** a problem, or someone is **raised** from a mineshaft, meaning lifted up. A building which is **razed** (often, **razed** to the ground) is flattened, totally destroyed.

- The queen who **reigns** holds the **reins** of the horse when it **rains**.
- He **rapped** on the table with his knuckles (staccato tapping, hence the name for a type of music) but we were listening with **rapt** attention anyway. Meanwhile he **wrapped** a present.
- **Right** means not left, or **rights** as in human rights. **Rite** means ceremony, hence burial **rites** means having a ceremony. If you bought a plot of land in a cemetery, you would have burial **rights**, meaning the right to be buried. You could **write** a letter about it. But a person who writes plays is a **playwright** (from the verb to work – the only other use is wrought, as of gold, etc. and also **wheelwright**, **shipwright**).
- You follow a **route** to get somewhere. A **root** means the basis or beginning of something – root of a plant, root of a verb, root of a problem.
- They bought a boat at the **sale**, to **sail** away to their secret island.
- The **sight** (someone saw it) of the burial **site** (place) was scary. Lawyers intend to **cite** it (use it as an example) in the court case.
- Hamlet used to **scull** around the lake like a normal boy but after all the tragic events he prefers talking to a **skull**.
- You **sort** clothes into matching colours before washing. But the past tense of seek is **sought**. He **sought** to convince her that he should be given a better mark.
- The love **story** was set in a three-**storey** house.
- Even though she was in dire **straits** she made sure to **straight**en her hair, because she knew that her boss was up for a flirt. (NB **strait**jacket means it is narrow and confines someone.)
- Schoolchildren are **taught**; washing lines are **taut**; a legal term meaning a wrong is a **tort**.
- **They're** in **their** house over **there**.
- The king was **thrown** off the **throne**.
- The squirrel often **throws** his partner into a tree while in the **throes** of passion.
- The medical student searched in **vain** (unsuccessfully) for a **vein** from which to draw some blood.
- The best **way** to **weigh** yourself is with your eyes closed.
- You **wave** at someone in the crowd, and therefore a plan could be waved through the council (meaning passed with just a gesture). But you **waive** the rules, meaning you abandon the rules.
- You never know **whether** or not the **weather** reporter is right.
- **Who's** the man **whose** hat you stole?

DISCUSSION AND REVISION SENTENCES

There are errors in the following sentences; work out what they are:

> After the match the team all went together to the pub on the corner. Thinking that their friends would be there.
> Sprinkled with chocolate flakes, children love this ice cream.
> The new exhibition starts on Friday, but will run for three weeks.
> The final richness of colour and tone are added.
> Muzakkir's football skills were as advanced, if not more so, than Jon.
> Jeannette Dobson, the council leader refused to reveal details of the new development.
> Men prefer cooler offices than their female colleagues, says a survey.
> Combating breast cancer is a difficult and exhausting task to conquer.
> Unlike Jane, piano practice was a torture for Kevin.

The following groups of sentences mean different things; sort out the different meanings:

> She wanted to buy a little-used car.
> She wanted to buy a little used car.

> Shakespeare's play *Hamlet* is very gloomy.
> Shakespeare's play, *Hamlet*, is very gloomy.

> I only clean the kitchen with soapsuds on Thursdays.
> I clean only the kitchen with soapsuds on Thursdays.
> I clean the kitchen with only soapsuds on Thursdays.
> I clean the kitchen with soapsuds only on Thursdays.

SUBBING AND PRESENTATION: THE VIEW FROM THE BRIDGE

Christopher McKane, Executive Editor, The Times

So you've filed your story and you reckon it's a pretty good one – should be a page lead at least, maybe in contention for the splash. You went on the job with a photographer, who told you he'd got some good snaps to enhance it, although you never saw them because he'd sent them over to the picture desk before you'd started writing. You'd talked it up to the news editor, who wanted a line for his newslist and made no further comment beyond saying he needed the copy at once. You wrote 800 words to be sure the subs had enough copy to give it a really good show. When you rang in later on the mandatory check call a different news editor simply said it was 'fine'. So you went home and hoped for the best. The desk have got your mobile number if they need you, anyway.

Next morning you pick up the paper to read on the way in. You flick through the news pages – there are a lot of them in a quality compact – checking the big headlines. Where's your story? They must be mad! At last: it's got a good position at the top of Page 4, but that witty, well-rounded report has come down to 15 lines or, to be precise, 76 words. And why no byline? The final insult – it simply says, in brackets ('a staff reporter writes'). You start to realize what a long way it is from the laptop to the breakfast table. Where did it all go wrong?

Let's stop the presses and begin at the beginning. What is a newspaper? John Walter, the first proprietor of *The Times*, wrote on January 1 1785: 'A newspaper ought to be the Register of the times and faithful recorder of every species of intelligence.' That is still a pretty good description and a modern paper has space for lots of diverse 'intelligence'. As a 'quality' reporter, you might look askance at a *Sun* story starting: 'Troubled funnyman Michael Barrymore's star is still shining – we had feared he might be damaged goods, said *Celebrity Big Brother* bookmakers Ladbrokes.' But the modern *Times* doesn't consider itself superior to popular cultural values – the same day it ran biographies of the contestants so that its readers could resist the urge to tune in at 3 am 'to watch some bloke called Maggot – we're watching it, so you don't have to.'

So you don't really have to worry that the subject of your story will be in some way unsuitable for your paper – the newsdesk wouldn't have assigned you if they thought it was going to be spiked as soon as it landed. Presentation matters enormously. It's a bit like speed-dating – your story will be assessed very quickly and you have only a minute to make a good first impression before being accepted or discarded. Of course through no fault of yours the night editor may find a date later in the evening that he finds more attractive and throw you out.

How do you dress up your story to catch the eye of an editor battered by a 24-hour flood of information? For a news story, the intro is vital. You might, if you are an experienced senior 'writer', get away with a more languid start for a background news feature, but in general, nothing more irritates the horny-handed news copy-tasters than stories that don't get to the point fast. And a good test of that is: 'What's the headline?' If three or four experienced backbench journalists aren't immediately sure what the headline is, then the story badly needs re-writing or it may even be spiked on the brutal grounds that it doesn't pass the 'so what test'. Take a moment to stand back from your story and prioritize your main points.

Another certain way to alienate the production journalists who put the paper together is with simple spelling mistakes. If you can't spell Middlesbrough or Mitterrand correctly, you undermine your credibility as a reporter. Don't even think about relying on a spellcheck. Don't say 'I Googled his name to check' unless you want to be hit over the head with *Who's Who* (but of course the KnowUK online version of *Who's Who* is perfectly accurate). Incredibly, there are reporters at *The Times* with degrees in English who can't spell. That isn't a little quirk that is joked about or easily forgiven – it's pathetically unprofessional.

Use your paper's style guide: at *The Times* this is no longer the slim blue volume that I was issued with when I joined in 1974, which contains such gems in its Aviation section as 'airship – prefer to dirigible' and 'propeller – prefer to airscrew'. Nowadays the guide is online and constantly updated but it still tells you to avoid jargon and journalese as well as how to spell Ulrika Jonsson. And it still deplores the use of words such as bonanza and crunch.

The style in which *The Times* should be written is based on the traditional plain style of English prose. It should be simple and clear. Short sentences are easier to understand. The tone of *The Times* has always been calm and judicious. It is this professional tone – clear, to the point, impartial and sensible – which is one of the essential virtues of the prose style of this newspaper.

Wise and timeless words from William Rees-Mogg's preface to the 1970 edition. He had certainly read Ernest Hemingway's principles of news writing from the Kansas City *Star* style book: 'Use short sentences. Use short first paragraphs. Use vigorous English, not forgetting to strive for smoothness. Be positive, not negative.'

Don't overwrite. Some stories are worth only one par – overwriting is another bane of the subs' life. When *The Times* switched from broadsheet to compact format many reporters failed to realize that the natural length for a page lead fell from 900 words to 600. They still wrote 900 or even more. Don't abrogate all decisions about length. If the story is going to be cut anyway, wouldn't you want to be the person who cuts it?

Don't be a prima donna:

I am dismayed that someone decided to 'improve' my figures and by so doing made them totally wrong. Since the backbench obviously don't think I am numerate (and I know lots of journalists who aren't) it may be worth bearing in mind that I am a trained mathematician with a triple scholarship in maths from Cambridge who specialized in statistics and studied quantum relativity with Stephen Hawking.

Subbing mistakes do happen – and an impetuous broadside like this genuine example can cause long-term damage to a reporter's relationship with the people who actually put her stuff into the paper.

Or try this whinge:

The whole column was ruined. It happens to me every two or three years when some holiday-leave August part-time retard comes in and thinks that 1,300 words written in colloquial style needs to be turned into late Edwardian Rees-Moggian prose. The thought of it is going to ruin my weekend. I just need to talk to the chief sub, whoever that is [note that the author doesn't even know the name of the chief sub] and be assured that it was all a terrible mistake. Otherwise I can't file another word until I've had a brain bypass operation.

This sort of widely circulated email may seem to be amusing, but it's not endearing.

The relationship between reporters and sub-editors has always been tense. In most offices a kind of demilitarized zone exists between the two areas. I overheard Leon Pilpel, my first chief sub-editor on *The Times*, saying to a very senior political correspondent who complained about the handling of his copy: 'You get it, we cut it.' (So just shut up, he might have added.) Old-school night editors used to describe the reporters and picture desks as no more than service departments. But you can break down those barriers – try to think like a sub. They get tired of being asked outside the office 'what do you write about' and then being politely blanked when they explain that they are faceless editors. Subbing is an honourable craft.

These guidelines by *The Times*'s senior news revise sub are aimed at casual subs, but they apply equally to reporters. Think how a sub's heart would lift if the reporter had already considered some of these presentational opportunities and avoided some of these pitfalls:

> Think outside the box and imagine your story on the page. [All reporters at *The Times* have 'read access' to page layouts.] If your story is part of a package look at the other stories to avoid doubled or contradictory information. If there's a graphic, look at it when it's finished. Think about pictures and graphics – they can't be made at a moment's notice. Make friends with the picture editors and the graphics department. Think about fact boxes and quirky little sidebars, standfirsts and quotes.
>
> No copy should arrive in Revise with statistics that clearly do not add up; with the wrong use of compared to/with or like/such as, or quote marks in the wrong place or the word 'only' misplaced.
>
> Keep the copy clean and make sure that legal marks can be clearly understood.
>
> Use the bloody style guide.
>
> Read the paper. [It's the height of unprofessionalism to have to be told crushingly 'that was in the paper this morning – didn't you see it?']
>
> Some reporters think that arts and showbiz stories require less care. This is absurd as (a) we look really stupid if we can't spell an actor or a TV programme known to millions and (b) the laws of libel apply just as much to showbiz luvvies.
>
> Subs matter. No matter the size of the backbench, the best page layout in the world won't work if the copy is crap, and the worst of pages can be saved by a clever headline and a good read.

Back to your story that made only a lead brief. Don't just sit and stew and become defensive. Read the rest of the paper. Yesterday your story was the centre of your world. God knows, you got cold, tired and hungry getting it, and the managing editor's new drive on expenses means that you can't even claim that Texaco sandwich and cup of hot coffee. Be realistic: there turned out to be several better stories around which you didn't know about at the time. Look carefully at how it was subbed – far too few reporters bother to compare their original copy with the published version. Learn from the online version too – almost all papers have an online section and the approach to subbing and presentation will be different from the printed version. Read the other papers to see what they made of it.

You might even pluck up courage and pick your moment to approach the backbench and ask the night editor what he thought of it. A bit of charm and diplomacy will get through his apparent crusty and world-weary exterior – the days of supercilious tyrants are gone. Very few reporters cross that line and get a toehold in the engine-room of the paper; many don't even know the subs' names, let alone have any relationship with them. Of course you know your news editors, but knowing the names and faces of those cynical subs who seem to do nothing but mutilate your words is vital. Find the noticeboard with the subs' rota on it and work out who does what and when they come in. Better still, go for a drink with them.

Subs are human too: they're disappointed when their headline is changed by the backbench or when the revise sub shouts 'five minutes all copy' and the story they have just picked up to sub has to go through with only the lightest polish and no fact checking. That's when clean copy from you scores highly and your accuracy really pays off. Never assume that facts will be checked for you; never write 'subs please check' unless you are filing from outer space with no access to reference sources. Even then, you'd do better not to write anything that you can't be certain is correct. When in doubt, leave it out.

Brilliant soloists writing superbly crafted columns grace the comment and feature pages, but writing for the news pages, producing that 'first rough draft of history' as Philip L. Graham of the *Washington Post* defined news, is a team game and always up against deadline. You can't hold back your copy until it has attained perfection – and even then, it would be perfect only in your eyes. Only in an ideal world will you be able to follow Leon Pilpel's advice when I asked him how much longer I should spend checking a story. He replied that I should be able to put my hand on my heart and say I had checked every fact before sending the copy down to the composing room. A time comes when you have to go with what you've got, and the cleaner and more accurate your copy is, the better its chance of surviving its rapid progression through many pairs of hands without even more errors being introduced.

At least on a newspaper you have only one or maybe two edition deadlines to file to, unless you're working on an election night, for example, when updated editions follow each other at a bewildering pace. At 4 am on an election morning when you find you can no longer keep up the pace, you'll agree with Douglas Adams when he said: 'I love deadlines. I like the whooshing sound they make as they fly by.' But if you're working for a news agency there's never any let-up. The Associated Press careers website says stirringly: 'Because we supply content to newspapers, broadcasters and websites in every time zone, we don't have set deadlines – every minute of every day is our deadline.'

When I went for my first job interview, on the weekly *Oxford Times*, I asked the editor whether the pace of work was very hectic. How patronizingly I smiled later when I remembered him replying that it could be pretty busy 'when the push is on'. Press day on a weekly paper? Busy?

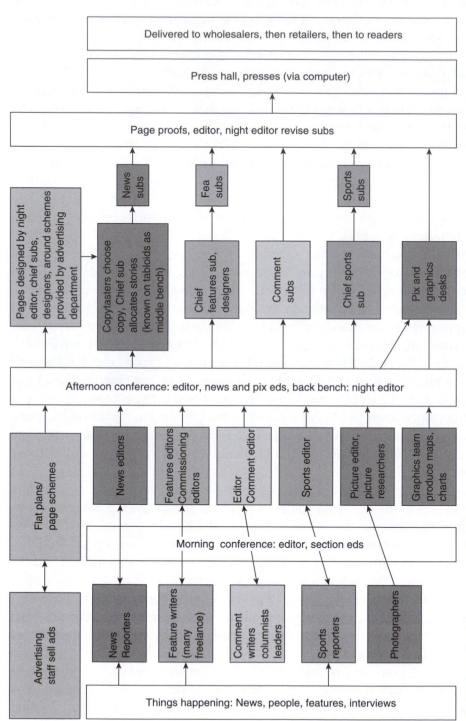

Figure 5 Flow chart for a newspaper story

Delivered to wholesalers, then retailers, then to readers

Press hall, presses (via computer)

Page proofs, editor, night editor revise subs

News subs

Fea subs

Sports subs

Pages designed by night editor, chief subs, designers, around schemes provided by advertising department

Copytasters choose copy, Chief sub allocates stories (known on tabloids as middle bench)

Chief features sub, designers

Comment subs

Chief sports sub

Pix and graphics desks

Afternoon conference: editor, news and pix eds, back bench: night editor

Flat plans/ page schemes

News editors

Features editors Commissioning editors

Editor Comment editor

Sports editor

Picture editor, picture researchers

Graphics team produce maps, charts

Morning conference: editor, section eds

Advertising staff sell ads

News Reporters

Feature writers (many freelance)

Comment writers columnists leaders

Sports reporters

Photographers

Things happening: News, people, features, interviews

The push? But every edition, every issue of every paper, has a deadline, and that's the fun of journalism – there's always a deadline and always another day to have another go.

Once in a while, do what I do after a long day in the office. Go home via the press hall. One of the subs or the production team – your new friends – will take you. There, work has barely begun – the 'lift' won't be until 4.30 or 5 am. It sounds hopelessly sentimental, but to see, hear and smell a press running and then hold a copy of the paper that you helped to create, is pure romance. Harry Evans said: 'Newspaper printing is a primitive business, noisy, messy and uncertain in comparison to electronic journalism, but there is an irreplaceable satisfaction in seeing the discrete copies of the paper emerge, a crystallization of mind and mechanics.'

Some of the magic of print, along with the fresh ink, will rub off on you. You might even decide, having mastered news writing, that you want to become a sub!

Figure 5 shows the way news about an event or a reporter's idea for a story makes its way from original conception to the moment when it appears on a page. The different stages the story goes through will vary according to the size of the paper and the resources it has. This chart shows roughly how things would be on a national newspaper. While all the same procedures will be followed on a small local paper or a magazine, on these publications many of the different tasks would be done by the same person. The news editor might write some stories, maybe on a weekly the news editor might also lay out a few pages as press day approaches. The editor may also lay out pages, and will almost certainly take the role of chief revise sub. There will probably not be a copytaster because almost all the material which arrives with the news editor will get into the paper.

OTHER MODELS USED ON NEWS PAGES

There are a number of other ways in which news is presented in papers and magazines apart from the single story about an event as described in previous chapters. Sometimes the same news needs to be presented twice, once for the front page, and again inside. Sometimes there is extra material that doesn't fit into the main story. Sometimes a great deal of disparate material from different places needs to be combined in one story.

THE WRITE-OFF

This is a truncated version of a story for the front page, when the events are covered in more detail inside. If there is a lengthy story which the editors decide is going to lead the paper, it may well not fit on the front, especially if there is a dramatic picture with it. They have two choices: (a) to start the story on the front and turn to an inside page or (b) to use a write-off: a self-contained story of perhaps 80 to100 words, which stands alone and gives the main points, and ends with a cross-reference to fuller coverage inside.

Here is the write-off from the front page of *The Times* on December 27 2004.

> The death toll passed 11,000 and was rising rapidly last night after one of the strongest earthquakes on record sent giant waves crashing over the coastlines of southern Asia.
>
> From its epicentre near the northwestern tip of Indonesia the underwater quake sent the 30ft-high tsunamis racing across the ocean until they smashed without warning into Sri Lanka, India, Thailand, Burma, Malaysia and Sumatra. The low-lying Maldive, Andoman and Nicobar islands were inundated. Sri Lanka was the worst-hit country, with 4,500 dead. One news bulletin (above) showed people clinging to the tops of buildings as water raged around them.

Across the region, tourists, many of them Britons, saw their resorts turned into disaster zones. In all, a million people were forced from their homes. The quake had a magnitude of 8.9, making it the fifth strongest since measurements began in 1899.

There were then about 10 more pages inside covering every aspect of the story. But notice that all the main points are here, and the story is related to the picture above it, since it serves as a caption as well. There are the facts of the quake, and where it happened. But there is also dramatic writing, with plenty of listen-to-me words: waves crashing, tsunamis racing, clinging, raged, forced from their homes.

It is chilling to note that the death toll, which seemed so high when it was first reported that day, turned out to be 20 times higher.

THE SIDEBAR OR BOX

There are several names for this. Sometimes it is called a box, or breakout box, or fact box, or the material might be boxed off. It means a smaller, related story on the same issue. Boxes used to appear mainly in features, when it was felt that a long feature needed some of the material presented separately to add interest to the page. They are used increasingly on news pages as well, as another way for the reader to enter the page. These secondary stories are often actually displayed in a ruled-off box, and on a tint background.

Sidebars to news stories include all sorts of different information. Sometimes they are chronologies: the *Guardian* labels these the 'back story', an expression from the world of drama and novel writing.

They can be used to give additional facts, such as ways to avoid a stroke in a story about the latest statistics for strokes, or even a couple of yoga positions in a story about sciatica. The tabloids often go for slightly funny ones: 'Ten things you didn't know about Norwich'. Sometimes a box is used for a different but related story: for example if a minister is involved in a political row, and there is a separate and unrelated story about the same department being criticized by a select committee.

The Times uses sidebars frequently on its news pages, partly because the compact size means that often there is room for only one longer story on a page. The sidebar is an extra way to catch the reader's eye.

THE ADD

Sometimes, when a newsworthy event happens in one place, some other very much smaller but related event happens somewhere else. The reporter at the second event might therefore file an add. Let's say for example an announcement is made about a new runway at Heathrow. There will be lots of material giving the announcement and the reaction, and then perhaps the London mayor might give a one-sentence quote about it during a meeting on another issue. The reporter might file that one sentence as an add to the main story. It might be woven in by the sub or it might be added to the bottom of the story, possibly with a bullet or blob. Some journalists describe this as 'blobbing it onto the bottom'.

BACKGROUNDERS

I feel it is unnecessary to reproduce a long backgrounder here. The Sunday papers are full of them, as are the dailies when there is a big news story which needs interpretation. A backgrounder might be a chronology of events which led up to the present situation, or it might be a narrative story of the same events which have made the main news story. When major court cases end, the papers often run big backgrounders of the whole affair, with profiles of the victim, the perpetrators, and details about the police investigation and so on.

THE WRAP

Often on national newspapers or big regionals a reporter is called upon to combine several stories in one, probably to go on to the front page. Sometimes this is a story with political developments in several countries, say perhaps in London and Brussels for an EU story, or London and Washington for a diplomatic story. Correspondents in several places file stories from their patches, and a reporter or sub has to make them into one coherent whole. This is a very common task at a news agency. Such a story is usually called a wrap on a newspaper, and a lead-all at an agency.

The most common type of wrap is a weather story. If there have been storms, strong winds or snow across the country, there might be a number of newsworthy incidents from all over the place. The journalist compiling the wrap needs to assemble this material to give the overall picture across the country (for a national) or across the area for a big regional paper.

The way to do this is to sit back far enough from the story to see the big picture. It is very much the opposite of the approach you would use if you were reporting a speech or extracting a story out of a document. In these cases the reporter homes in on the most interesting point, and simply leaves out some of the others, to avoid the pizza effect (see Chapter 4).

If you are compiling a wrap you might of course have to leave out a number of inessentials, but you must provide information about all the significant events. A wrap story is therefore inevitably a bit like a pizza, with lots of very different items brought together. The skill for the sub or reporter is to merge all the ingredients into a well-made report.

SCENARIO 1: COMPILING A WRAP FOR A STORM STORY

Here is some material which might have come into a newsdesk from staff reporters and agencies across the country after a storm. You are writing for a Midlands evening paper publishing on March 2.

Banbury, Oxfordshire, March 2

218 Banbury residents were moved from their homes last night and were accommodated in a school on the other side of town for the night after being evacuated from their homes which are flooded.

Jon Franklin, 54, of Risinghill Estate, Banbury, said: 'We were in bed when the police came round with loudspeakers, hammering on the door, saying the river had burst its banks. We just had time to find our boots and things, when the street started flooding. I couldn't believe it. We didn't have time to do anything. As we left, the water had reached our front door.'

PC Noel Thackleberry, who helped to evacuate residents, said: 'One old lady, who was disabled and couldn't walk, was lying in her bed screaming for help. We helped her out, and she is spending the night at the school. She was very scared, as the water had seeped into her house before we got to her.'

London, March 2

While thousands of people are still recovering from recent floods that caused millions of pounds worth of damage to homes and businesses, the plight of wildlife has been largely ignored. But conservation groups and farmers' representatives are beginning to estimate the scale of the damage. This includes hundreds of sheep swept to their death by floods, and countless smaller wild animals, such as hedgehogs and dormice, killed by the startling reverse of the weather. More disturbingly, signs of long-term changes in the climate are also being recorded, with implications for the countryside.

Evesham, Worcestershire, March 2

Two people were killed just outside Pershore late last night when their car was hit by a tree, which was uprooted in torrential rain. Peter Olley, 57, and his wife Julie, 52, were driving to their home in Pershore. Although the road they were using was not flooded, the fields nearby were waterlogged and an ash tree in a hedge next to the road was uprooted by a sudden gust of wind.

Motorists and anglers were rescued by RAF helicopters across Worcestershire, as the county experienced the brunt of yesterday's storms. Outside Evesham, John Barham, a 55-year-old farmer, was winched to safety from the roof of his Land-Rover when it was marooned while crossing a bridge.

Droitwich, Worcestershire March 1
Floodwater completely cut off the town of Droitwich for a time today, and the hotels are fully booked by stranded motorists. Police arranged for some stranded motorists to spend tonight in spare rooms in The Limes, an elderly persons' residential care home in the town.

Worcester, March 1
Fears are growing for a local boy, Jamey Pederson, 15, who has been missing since this morning, when he set out to do his paper round. His bike has been found in the swollen river Severn, near where it had burst its banks to the south of the city. Police said the body of a teenage boy had been found in the river three miles downstream of the city.

Upton upon Severn, Worcestershire March 1
Police appealed to the public today to provide boats to help with rescue operations. Soldiers and volunteer civilian divers helped evacuate people from their homes. Hope is fading for a 33-year-old woman who fell from a cabin cruiser into the Severn this morning. Mrs Joan Braceridge, who lives near Upton, had gone to check on the family's boat, which was moored on the river near the town centre. According to eyewitnesses, the boat lurched as the river rose, and she lost her footing. An RAF helicopter was searching for her during the afternoon, but abandoned the search as darkness fell.

London, March 2
More rain is forecast for today and tomorrow as a deep Atlantic depression moves across Britain. Last night 28 flood warnings were issued, mostly in the Midlands and central England. Melting snow and heavy rain followed the icy wintry weather that has gripped the country for the past week. The floods are expected to be as serious this week as those which swept the country last November.

Winsham, Somerset, March 1
Two people were rescued by an RAF helicopter today. One man was plucked to safety from the roof of his car and another was lifted from a tree he climbed to escape the water.

Tewkesbury, March 2
Three people were rescued from rising floodwater in Gloucestershire after the driver of a stranded car called the emergency services on his mobile phone when the vehicle stalled in waist-deep water near Tewkesbury. Soldiers and council workers were out in force in the town today, lining streets with sandbags as levels on the river Severn continued to rise. More storms are forecast in the area on Monday.

Parts of an £8 million Severn flood protection scheme, built after the previous highest levels in 1982, were being breached. Residents were told to move belongings upstairs and 'prepare for the worst'. Town councillors, Environment Agency staff, emergency services and Army representatives held a crisis summit today, as a further five severe flood warnings were issued for the area by the Environment Agency. John Prentice, the Deputy Prime Minister, met flood defence workers in Tewkesbury. He also visited Bristol and Upton upon Severn, Worcestershire. There, he waded through thigh-high water to visit the home of Sid Youngson, which had been flooded for the second time in 18 months. Mr Youngson said afterwards: 'It was a bit of a public relations stunt but at least he has seen my house. He said he will be able to picture it in his mind in the future.' Mr Youngson said: 'I am gutted with what has happened. I thought the first time was a one-off and then it happened again less than two years later.'

A man was killed at Maudlin, near Bodmin, Cornwall, when his Ford Sierra struck a wall on an icy country road. Waters from the Axe river in Devon washed away a bridge on the A358 and a fireman was rescued when he became stranded by fast-flowing water.

Seven flood warnings were in force on rivers in Dorset and Somerset including the Yeo, Frome, Stour, Bride and upper Parrett. Similar warnings were in force in East Sussex and West Sussex for the Lavant, Ems, Adur and Cuckmere. Warnings in central England applied to the Avon upstream of Rugby and between Evesham and Tewkesbury, in Gloucester, and also to the River Trent.

Here is a version of a wrap story based on the material above.

Five people are feared dead after storms swept Britain yesterday, rivers burst their banks and communities were cut off by floodwater.

Para 1: The intro sums up all the important events – the death toll, and the drama of the rivers bursting their banks and people being stranded.

The worst-hit area was the West Midlands, where two people were killed when their car hit an uprooted tree, and two others, one a 15-year-old boy, are believed to have been swept away by the swollen river Severn.

Para 2: Homes in on the worst-hit area, and gives more detail on the deaths, which are the most dramatic points of the story.

A man was killed at Maudlin, near Bodmin, Cornwall, when his car struck a wall on an icy country road.

Para 3: If you write five deaths in the intro, you must be sure that the detail in your story adds up correctly.

Floodwater cut off the town of Droitwich for a time and stranded motorists spent the night in spare rooms in a residential care home.

Paras 4–5: Two of the most dramatic points – people evacuated from their homes.

In Banbury 218 residents were evacuated from their flooded homes to a school on the other side of town for the night.

Jon Franklin, 54, of Risinghill Estate, said: 'We were in bed when the police came round with loudspeakers, hammering on the

Paras 6–7: The all important quotes. These are the best quotes we have got. If we had quotes about the people who were killed, we would have put those here.

door, saying the river had burst its banks. We just had time to find our boots and things, when the street started flooding. I couldn't believe it. We didn't have time to do anything. As we left, the water had reached out front door.'

PC Noel Thackleberry, who helped to evacuate residents, said: 'One old lady, who was disabled and couldn't walk, was lying in her bed screaming for help. We helped her out, and she is spending the night at the school. She was very scared, as the water had seeped into her house before we got to her.'

Two people were killed just outside Pershore when their car was hit by a tree, which was uprooted in torrential rain. Peter Olley, 57, and his wife Julie, 52, were driving to their home in the town. Although the road was not flooded, the fields nearby were waterlogged and an ash tree in the hedge was torn up by a sudden gust of wind.

Paras 8–10: Details about the deaths. It is reasonable to assume that these people are lost, as it is now 24 hours since the events, and if you have reliable stringers in the area, you can assume that you would have heard if either had been found alive.

Motorists and anglers were rescued by RAF helicopters across Worcestershire as the county took the brunt of the storms. Outside Evesham, John Barham, 55, a farmer, was winched to safety from the roof of his Land Rover when it was marooned while crossing a bridge.

In Worcester, fears are growing for a local boy, Jamey Pederson, 15, who has been missing since yesterday morning, when he set out on his paper round. His bike has been found in the Severn, near where it had burst its banks south of the city. Police said the body of a teenage boy had been found in the river three miles downstream of the city.

At Upton upon Severn, police appealed to the public for boats to help with rescue operations. Soldiers and volunteer civilian divers helped to evacuate people from their homes. Hope is fading for a 33-year-old woman who fell from a cabin cruiser into the Severn yesterday morning. Joan Braceridge, who lives near Upton upon Severn, had gone to check on her family's boat, which was moored on the river near the town centre. Eyewitnesses said the boat lurched as the river rose, and she lost her footing. An RAF helicopter abandoned the search for her as darkness fell.

Paras 11–13: *Details of other dramatic events.*

Another RAF helicopter rescued two people at Winsham in Somerset. One man was plucked to safety from the roof of his car and another was lifted from a tree he had climbed to escape the water.

Three people were saved from rising floodwater in Gloucestershire after the driver of a stranded car called the emergency services on his mobile phone when the vehicle stalled in waist-deep water near Tewkesbury.

Soldiers and council workers were out in force in the town today, lining streets with sandbags as the Severn continued to rise.

Parts of an £8 million Severn flood protection scheme, built after the previous highest levels in 1982, were breached. Residents of Tewkesbury were told to move belongings upstairs and 'prepare for the worst'.

Councillors, Environment Agency staff, emergency services and Army representatives were holding a crisis summit today, as a further five severe flood warnings were issued for the area by the Environment Agency.

James Prentice, the Deputy Prime Minister, met flood defence workers in Tewkesbury. At Upton upon Severn, he waded through thigh-high water to visit the home of Sid Youngson, which had been flooded for the second time in 18 months. Mr Youngson said afterwards: 'It was a bit of a public relations stunt but at least he has seen my house. He said he will be able to picture it in his mind in the future.' Mr Youngson added: 'I am gutted with what has happened. I thought the first time was a one-off and then it happened again less than two years later.'

Waters from the river Axe in Devon washed away a bridge on the A358 and a fireman was rescued when he became stranded by fast-flowing water.

Paras 14–17: Having got all the main drama in, we now have some up-to-the-minute material about what is happening today, always good for an evening paper. Some more good quotes, and some political detail.

More rain is forecast for today and tomorrow as a deep Atlantic depression moves across Britain. Last night 28 flood warnings were issued, mostly in the Midlands and central England. Melting snow and heavy rain followed the icy wintry weather that has gripped the country for the past week. The floods are expected to be as serious this week as those which swept the country last November.

Paras 19: Story ends with up-to-date information about weather conditions, and flood warnings.

THE RUNNING OR BREAKING STORY

Reporters and subs at news agencies and at web news providers often have to write a story during a series of events, and then update it as more information arrives. This is known as a running or breaking story. It is usual to **re-top** the story as and when there is an important development. The agency will provide a new first few paragraphs and then write 'pick up previous' or 'pick up tiger 1 London'. Then from time to time the whole story will be written through again, and 'no pick-up' will appear at the end to indicate to the subscribers that they now have a completely new story. Journalists providing material for a web page have a slightly different task – not only must they produce a complete new story every time they write an update, but it must also make a specific number of words.

Again, as when writing a wrap story, it is important to sit far enough back from the story to assess the most important points. If new information arrives, you have to decide quickly if it is better than the material in your first few paragraphs. You also need to consider whether the sources can be trusted. If you work for a big newspaper or agency in London for example, taxi drivers sometimes ring in with an interesting thing they say has happened, but you must remember that they might be wrong. When we do these exercises with students we always put in bits of information from possibly unreliable sources, to see whether they can spot them.

SCENARIO FOR DISCUSSION

Here is a lot of information which might have come into a news provider. It could be written up into six or seven different stories, as new information arrives. Think about which bits of drama and action you want to get at the top of each story, and beware of rumour and possibly libellous material.

Marianne, the rock singer involved in the story, is very famous, so most newspapers would want to publish as much as possible about her in the story, even though there is a legal danger. It is essential to get as many lively quotes in as possible and to source your quotes correctly to named people. This gives the story weight and authenticity.

The way to do this type of story is to write the first one, and then use that as the basis for the second, weaving material in at the top as you go along. Each story should be written as if your reader is coming to it new. Only in a completely new news cycle, say the next day, should you assume that your reader knows something about it.

SCENARIO 2: SIMBA ESCAPES

A member of the public telephones you:

'A tiger has escaped from London Zoo. I was walking in Regent's Park, when I suddenly realized that several police cars with sirens were arriving. Suddenly there were zoo keepers all over the place, and police pushing people away.

There was a tiger just at the side of the zoo buildings by the road through the park. I suddenly saw it. I was so scared I nearly fell over. It looked very dopey. I don't know whether it was sedated or something. Workmen came with huge screens. I just ran away, I didn't see where it went.

My name is Barbra Smythe. I'm 27 and I work for Camden Council in the finance department. I had a day off and had been sunbathing in the park. This is really scary. I can't imagine how it can have happened.'

You ring the zoo press office and a spokesman, who refuses to give his name, says:

'I can confirm that a tiger which was having a routine operation in the veterinary wing to the north of the Outer Circle road has escaped from the unit. The tiger is Simba, a five-year-old female. She was having an operation on an impacted tooth. It seems she woke up from the anaesthetic sooner than expected, taking the vets and keepers by surprise.

The whole area has been cordoned off. There is no danger to the public. Police marksmen have been called in to sedate her again with a tranquilizing dart.'

In response to questions, the spokesman adds:

'This is the first time something like this has happened in my memory. Occasionally one of the pet animals makes its way out of the enclosed children's corner, and is quickly returned. But a big cat getting loose has never happened in recent times to my knowledge. We have strict emergency procedures laid down though, and they were all followed to the letter. Simba is not moving very quickly, as she is still suffering the effects of the anaesthetic, and she is very near the veterinary unit. We expect to return her to her pen very soon. There is no danger at all.'

You talk to Scotland Yard's press office:

'Police are attending an incident in Regent's Park where apparently a tiger has escaped. We have sent squad cars and police marksmen are on their way. We have no further information at this point.'

You happen to have a friend, Frances Maddox, a 30-year-old freelance webmaster, who lives in St Mark's Rise, just north of Regent's Park near the zoo. You telephone her. She says: 'I've been hearing police sirens and everything for the past hour. I didn't know what was going on.' She looks out of her window while talking to you.

'The whole area around the vets' block seems to have been cordoned off. It all seems to be deserted. I can't see any tiger. I can see what looks like police with shields and body armour the other side of the screens. If there is a tiger loose, they don't seem to know where it is. Some of them are looking around with binoculars. There are high screens along the pavement, which I can see from here.'

The phone rings again. It is another member of the public:

'Did you know that a tiger has escaped from the zoo? It has got down on to the canal towpath, and is making its way towards Little Venice.

My name is Christophe Lafleur. I'm 27, I'm French and I'm studying computer science at Imperial College. I was jogging along the path just by Regent's Park when suddenly two police officers raced up behind me and told me to go back the other way. They said a tiger had escaped. Is that true? I can't believe it.

There are two helicopters overhead, and I can hear sirens. I'm heading back the other way towards Camden, but I don't know how I am going to get home. I live in Kilburn.'

You ring the zoo's press office again, and speak to Jenifer Baddeen. She is the chief press officer.

'I can confirm that Simba, a five-year-old female tiger which was in the veterinary wing to the north of the Outer Circle road, has escaped from the unit. She was having an operation on an impacted tooth, and woke up from the anaesthetic sooner than the vets expected.

It now appears that before she could be recaptured, she made her way down on to the Regent's Canal. She is believed to be moving west towards Little Venice. Police have evacuated everyone who was on that stretch of canal, and the whole section has been sealed off. Police marksmen are standing by to sedate her again with a tranquilizing dart, when we can locate her.

According to our records this is the first time something like this has happened in modern times. Our emergency procedures were followed, but unfortunately Simba had disappeared before we could sedate her again.'

Another member of the public rings in.

'Is it true that Marianne has been attacked by a tiger? I often see her jogging along the canal with her bodyguards. She lives in Little Venice doesn't she?

I work in the coffee shop in Little Venice, just by the canal. It's called the Café Fenice. Someone who came in told me they saw her getting into an ambulance just down the road from here. She looked OK apparently, she was walking.'

You ring Scotland Yard. A spokesman says:

'We have approximately 50 officers searching for a tiger which has escaped from London Zoo. It is believed to be on the canal towpath just west of Regent's Park. Our officers are well protected with riot shields and body armour. We also have two helicopters searching, but have been unable to locate the animal as yet. We have no information about any casualties.'

A taxi driver rings you:

'You are not going to believe this mate, but apparently Marianne has shot a tiger at London Zoo. At least that's the rumour. Is it true?'

You ring a friend in the control room of the ambulance service.

'Yes, off the record it is true that we have collected Marianne and taken her to the Wellington Hospital. But apparently she isn't injured. She is just in shock. Is it true about a tiger?'

You talk to a contact in the Met:

'Apparently we have arrested two men on the canal. They are believed to work for Marianne. I'm not sure why, something about firearms.'

You ring the Wellington Hospital:

'We can confirm that Marianne is here and is seeing doctors. She is unlikely to be admitted.'

Meanwhile your contact at Café Fenice rings again:

'Have you heard? Apparently Marianne's bodyguards shot the tiger. That's dreadful isn't it? There are police and zoo keepers and ambulances and things all over the place here. I can't see what is going on though. They have told me to close the café and stay inside. They have turned everyone off the streets.'

You ring the zoo's press office again. Jenifer Baddeen says:

'We have located Simba and are making arrangements to get her back to the zoo. She is believed to be injured, and had fallen into the canal. She has managed to get herself out, but we are still trying to sedate her enough to approach her. If she is injured, she will be angry, and therefore more dangerous. When we can sedate her we will be able to use a hoist, which we have brought to the towpath nearby, to get her on to a stretcher and into an animal ambulance.'

You ring Scotland Yard again. A press officer says:

'Two men are helping us with our inquiries following an incident on the Regent's Canal this afternoon. We expect to bring charges. I cannot give any further details.'

Your contact in the Met confirms that two men are being questioned about firearms offences.

Scotland Yard issues another statement:

We have recaptured a tiger which escaped from London Zoo earlier today.

It has been sedated and is now being returned to the zoo by animal ambulance. We believe the animal was injured in an incident which we are investigating. I cannot give any further information at this stage.

FURTHER POINTS FOR DISCUSSION

You have been given information 'off the record'. Strictly speaking you should not use this unless you get a second source that confirms the information. But you've had two reports mentioning Marianne. You can write with confidence that she was involved in some way, or you can play safe and say something like: 'believed or reported to be involved, according to unconfirmed reports'.

Marianne is so famous she should be in the intro, but the reference should probably be qualified by saying something like 'according to unconfirmed reports'. Your contact said 'apparently she is not injured' so you can't be certain she was attacked.

The report from the taxi driver that 'apparently Marianne has shot a tiger' seems so unlikely it is unsafe to use this. Work on the basis of 'if in doubt, leave it out'.

For later stories you can tell us that the men are being questioned but you need to be very careful about giving any more information about them, since at any minute they may be charged.

EPILOGUE

When there is nothing else left to say the best news stories just stop (see the inverted pyramid diagram on page 47). I have reached the end of the points I wanted to make, so that's it. I will just add that news reporting is very good fun. There is a basic human satisfaction in finding something out that other people don't know, and then telling them. And writing it well, so that everyone can easily see the story, and indeed so the subs don't need to do much to it, is very interesting and very satisfying, especially with your name at the top of it.

Good luck with it.

FURTHER READING

If you want to become good at writing news stories, you must read a lot of good news stories. Read lots of different publications, and try to read several versions of the same story, to work out how the reporters have treated the story differently. For straight clear stories the BBC website is very good. The *Daily Mail* is the best for well-written, slightly unusual treatments of news stories. The *Sun* and the *News of the World* are very good for seeing how clear stories can be written in the shortest number of words. The *Guardian* often has a much more reflective approach, and it is interesting to compare its approach with that of other papers.

BIBLIOGRAPHY

Galtung, J., and Ruge, M.H. (1965) 'The Structure of Foreign News', *The Journal of International Peace Research.*

Journalism: A Career Handbook, Anna McKane (A&C Black, 2004) describes in detail all the different jobs in print journalism and how to get them.

Essential English, Harold Evans (Pimlico, 2000) is an in-depth study of how to write for newspapers. It may be very slightly outdated.

Bryson's Dictionary of Troublesome Words: A Writer's Guide to Getting it Right, Bill Bryson (Broadway, 2004) is an entertaining read and is invaluable for anyone who wants to be sure they have got the correct word for something. Bryson was a sub-editor on *The Times* and the *Independent* before he became a best-selling author.

The Elements of Style, William Strunk and E. B. White (newest edition by Penguin, 2005). Don't be put off by the fact that this was first written in 1918. It is beautifully written, and still the clearest and most concise guide to writing. However, it has its detractors.

Spunk & Bite: A Writer's Guide to Punchier, More Engaging Language and Style, Arthur Plotnik (Random House, 2005) attacks Strunk as being too prescriptive.

The Complete Plain Words, Ernest Gowers (Penguin, 1987) and *Modern English Usage,* Henry Fowler (Oxford 2002) are such classics that they are often simply referred to as Fowler or Gowers. They are both well written and interesting to read, but I fear they have been overtaken by the many changes in usages in the last few years.

Eats, Shoots and Leaves: the Zero Tolerance Approach to Punctuation, Lynne Truss, (Profile, 2003) sets out the main punctuation rules and is funny as well.

English for Journalists, Wynford Hicks (Routledge, 1998) gives guidance on grammar, jargon and word economy. There are other short books in the same series on interviewing and subbing.

The Newspapers Handbook, Richard Keeble (Routledge, 2001) and *The Magazines Handbook* by Jenny McKay (Routledge, 2000) both give a lot of information about these sections of the industry, and both cover writing as well.

Print Journalism: A Critical Introduction, edited by Richard Keeble (Routledge, 2005) gives an overview of all aspects of print journalism by lecturers in each area.

It is a good idea to read some books by journalists, either collected published pieces, such as Julie Burchill's or Jeffrey Bernard's, books about reporting assignments, such as Robert Fisk's or John Simpson's, or those based on specific ideas, such as Fran Abrams on poverty. Granta publishes collections of journalism. As well as giving you an idea of the range of work that journalists do, it will give you something to talk about in interviews.

WEBSITES

www.bbc.co.uk for clear concise news writing.

www.plainenglish.co.uk for useful advice and interesting extracts from poor writing. Their idea is that official documents should be clear enough to be understood at one reading: exactly the same as journalism should be.

www.poynter.org is the site of the journalism school at St Petersburg, Florida. There is a lot of interesting material on the site, in particular the section 'Writing tools from the workbench of Roy Peter Clark'.

GLOSSARY

add   extra material from a different reporter which will be added to a story

angle   the viewpoint from which a reporter writes a story. Papers with different political stances will often take very different angles on the same story

article   this expression is never used by journalists; they talk about a story, or a piece, or about *copy*

backbench   the senior production team, including chief sub, copytaster and revise sub. Tabloids often have *middle benches* as well, grouping senior people responsible for different editions

background   essential material which needs to be in a story to enable the reader to understand how the event came about

backgrounder   extra story with background material, which would appear with the main story

beat   see *specialism*

Berliner   the medium size for a newspaper adopted by the *Guardian* and the *Observer*

blob   see *bullet*

box, breakout box   a secondary story with some extra information, which relates to the main story. It is often presented in a panel, or box, perhaps with a tinted background. Also called side-bar, fact box

breaking story   see *running story*

brief   details given to reporters, feature writers or photographers to enable them to start work on a story

broadsheet   the larger size of newspaper used now only by the *Financial Times* and the *Daily Telegraph*

bullet or blob   black dot, star or square either used to set out several points within a news story, or to add a related point at the bottom, when it might be said to be a blob par, or to be blobbed on

business to business or B2B   magazines about a particular industry, for the people who work in it

byline   the name of the writer of a story

catchline   single word that identifies a story to enable it to be traced in the system

chief sub   the leader of the team of sub-editors, who assigns stories to the *down-table subs* to edit

clunk   my expression for a sudden shock or surprise for the reader at the end of a sentence or paragraph. It is often used to great effect in features or quirky news stories

colour story   one which gives a word picture of a place or event

compact   the description used by the *Independent* and now *The Times* to describe their new size, to distinguish themselves from the tabloids

conference   meeting that takes place once or twice a day on a newspaper, or less often on a weekly or monthly magazine, to discuss what stories are available, to monitor progress and perhaps review the previous issue

consonance   the expression used by Galtung and Ruge to illustrate their theory that people like to read stories which fit in with what they expect to happen

contacts   people who make news (councillors, headteachers, leaders of pressure groups etc.) whom a reporter gets to know so that they might supply her with information. All their details are kept in a contacts book, which should also be backed up elsewhere in case it gets lost

copy   collective term for material written by a reporter

copy-taster   senior *sub-editor* or *backbench* person who looks at all incoming copy and chooses what will be used in the publication or on the agency's wire

cross-reference   line at the bottom of a story drawing the reader's attention to related material elsewhere

curtain raiser   forward-throwing story written before an event

cuttings   the previous stories about an issue, now held electronically. Also known as **cuts**. The word also refers to the copies of published stories which a journalist keeps in a portfolio

diary   used to be a big desk diary, but is probably now kept in the computer system with details of all events which might make a story. Diary also refers to gossip or people columns

downtable subs   the rank and file *sub-editors* who edit copy at the request of the senior team

drop intro, delayed drop   a story where the most important point is left until the second or third paragraph, to make for a more colourful start to the story. Often used on quirky or funny stories

exclusive   a story that no other publication has got – a scoop

fact box   see *box*

feature   this has come to cover everything which is not on the news pages. So it would include everything from an investigation into MRSA in hospitals to an astrology column

file   the act of sending a story. Reporters file to the newsdesk, and agencies file stories to their subscribers

filing editor, filer   a senior journalist at an agency who sends the copy to the subscribers, putting it on the *wire*. He or she is in effect the *revise sub*

filler   short story used to fill up a gap in the page

first person piece   this would generally be an eye-witness account, or a piece of colour writing about an event, written from the point of view of the reporter. It is not quite the same as a column, which would generally appear regularly

five Ws   Who, What, Why, Where, When, the checklist for the reporter to make sure she has covered all the basics of a news story

flash   the fastest, briefest dispatch from an agency used for a very important story. It will be followed almost immediately by a fuller version. See also *snap*

follow-up   a new story, with new material, written about something that was covered in a previous edition or rival publication

frequency   the term used by Galtung and Ruge to show that for a story to be newsworthy it has to have happened since the publication last went to press

getting a quote   often a reporter rings up several people who might be able to add something to a story, to get more comments to make the story livelier

go to bed   extremely old-fashioned expression meaning when the publication is sent to the printers and nothing further can be changed

graphic   a diagram, drawing, chart or map, usually created on a computer, used to illustrate a story

greengrocer's apostrophe   an apostrophe used wrongly for a plural word, as often appears on market stalls – e.g. 'Ripe tomato's'

hack   journalist

handout   press release or other item from which a story might be written

headline   NEVER use the word title for the words at the top of a story. Journalists always call them the headline

heavies   the broadsheet or former broadsheet papers. The term used to refer to the type of story in them, but in the case of the Sundays, they are literally heavy

hole   journalists' expression for a vital piece of information which is missing from a story

house style or **style book**   certain word usages, spelling, punctuation etc., which a paper or magazine has fixed on, probably now held online. New recruits should refer to it regularly

insert   some copy that is put into a story later, perhaps for clarification

intro   the first paragraph of a news story

inverted pyramid   used to describe the traditional way of writing a news story, with the important information at the top, and then the rest of the material arranged in descending order of importance

kill   when a story the paper had planned to use is discarded, it is killed. Agencies use this expression on a urgent message if a story which has been issued proves to be incorrect

lead, lead story   the main story on page one of a newspaper, also known as the splash

lead-all   see *wrap*

lead brief   the top story of a column of news in brief items

listen-to-me words   my expression for arresting words which liven up a story, giving it colour and interest and making the reader want to read on

literal or typo   (typographical error) used to refer to errors made during printing. Since journalists are now responsible for the material as it appears in the paper, these are perhaps more realistically regarded as spelling errors

middle bench   see *back bench*

mug shot   head and shoulders front-facing photograph

newsdesk   either where the *news editor* works, or a collective term for several news editors

news editor   the person whose job it is to make sure stories are covered, assigning reporters, assessing the worth of stories, and liaising with the production team. Often called chief reporter on local papers, because in small teams this person will do some reporting

newslist   the list complied by the *news editor* of what stories she is planning to cover for the next edition

newsprint   the paper on which newspapers are printed

nib   news in brief, a column of short stories each probably about 50–80 words covering a number of different events

night editor   senior journalist on a morning paper who takes control when the editor goes home

nose   old-fashioned term for the intro to a story. To re-nose a story would involve writing a different intro

off-diary   stories which a reporter has found either through observation, or through talking to contacts, which she brings in to the *newsdesk*

off-the-record   refers to information which a source reveals on condition that it is not attributed to her

page lead   the main story on a newspage

par or **para**   paragraph

patch   an area which a reporter is assigned to cover. Generally a geographical area but it might be an area of news such as education or health. See also *specialism*

press release   announcement to the press, probably now released electronically

production editor   the person who coordinates the work of getting a publication to the printer

proof   a paper version of a page or pages produced for a final check

red top   tabloids such as the *Sun* that have red mastheads

re-jig   rewrite a story

reportage   descriptive writing or photography that gives the atmosphere and a picture of an event or situation

re-top   to update a story with new information that is important enough to be at the beginning of the story

revise sub   senior *backbench* person who checks copy before the page is finally passed

round-up   see *wrap*

running story or **breaking story**   usually for a web provider or an agency, a story which has to be rewritten several times as new information comes in

scoop   see *exclusive*

sell   see *standfirst*

sidebar   see *box*

slow burner   a story where the main news point is left until further down, and the piece is written in a very relaxed, probably narrative style. It works mainly with humorous stories

snap   agency term for a very brief item alerting subscribers to an event. It will be followed by a more detailed story. For the most dramatic event the agency will issue a *flash*

source   a contact who provides some information to go into a story, or a reference in a story to how the reporter knows about the information

specialism   an area such as education, politics, crime, which a reporter is assigned to cover, so that she gets to know the issues and people involved. This is known in the US as a beat

spike   in the days when copy was produced on paper a story was placed on a metal spike if it was not going to be used. If there was an inquiry about the story the spiked material could be checked. Some news rooms still have a folder or queue in the computer system which is labelled the spike

splash   see *lead*

standfirst   the one or two sentences often seen at the top of a feature, or a featurish news story, which is designed to encourage the reader into the story. Usually known in magazines as the sell

stringer   freelance who is paid a retainer to provide news as necessary

stylebook   see *house style*

sub-editor or **sub**   one of the team who checks stories for content, accuracy, legal pitfalls and style, cut them to length, and write headlines. Some will design pages

tabloid   the smaller format for newspapers, which until recently was a synonym for a more populist approach. This may alter since the change in size recently of the *Independent* and *The Times*

threshold   term used by Galtung and Ruge to show that the bigger the scale of the story, the more likely it is to become news

vox pops (vox populi)   brief interviews with random people, probably in the street, about an issue

washing-line   an expression used occasionally to describe a story which has a number of quotes or examples of fairly equal interest, so some of them could be removed from the middle of the story without losing any vital information

wire   agency term for its service. To wire means to send in material

wrap   a story which brings together a lot of material from different sources. Also called a lead-all (on agencies) or a round-up. It might be written by a reporter or on an agency by a senior sub

write-off   a short self-contained story on the front of a paper which sums up the main points of an event. There will be longer stories inside the paper

APPENDIX 1: NEWS STORIES IN THE NATIONAL PRESS, JULY 18/19 2005

The papers have been grouped alphabetically into the following groups: broadsheet or former broadsheet, mid-market, tabloids.

We made a separate group of the politics stories, to give an idea of how much each paper covered, but I see politics as a sub-group of conflict.

Note – we left out all the stories on the gossip/diary pages which appear in every paper on the grounds that they are more like a feature page about celebrities. Several months after they have appeared they all seem even more inconsequential than they did at first, and in a way they all cancel each other out. In a few cases papers have similar items, but on the whole, each paper has four or five totally different stories from those in rival papers, but they all fall into the category of very minor stories about celebs: Sophie Anderton has haircut, Jane Fonda didn't think much of *Easy Rider*, and so on.

MONDAY JULY 18

THE GUARDIAN

Page   *Story*

CONFLICT

Page	Story
1	London bombs Iraq link
1	Iraq suicide bombs
2	Spain forest fires
2	Iraq bombs (contd from page 1)
4	London bomber
4	London bombs bookshop
4	London bombs Egyptian chemist
5	London bombers picture
5	London bombs Pakistan links denied
5	London bombs victims
6	Turkey bomb blasts
12	Girl critical after arson attack

12   Man dies in boat accident
13   Israeli troops on Gaza border
13   Hurricane Emily
15   Iraq bombs – victims and pull out plans
15   Iraq Saddam trial set
15   Iraq Bush tried to aid parties
16   Tsunami aftermath
16   Tamil tigers warn of imminent war (nib)
16   1980s police killings confirmed in Guatemala (nib)

POLITICS

1   Edward Heath dies
2   White House advisers named in CIA leak
2   Energy-saving targets scrapped
3   Duncan Tory slur
10   Whitehall shuffle
11   Edward Heath tributes
12   Government censors foreign office Iraq book
12   Tolpuddle rally (nib)
13   Spain to buy land to protect coast from urbanisation
14   Indonesia/Aceh peace talks
16   New Jersey politician's apology for Hitler comment

CELEBS

1   Powerful in media list
3   Real Big Brother watched George Orwell
8   Camilla's coat of arms
9   Harry Potter launch

HUMAN INTEREST – RELEVANCE TO THE READER

8   BBC may sell programmes on internet (hard to categorize – we decided the main point was relevance to licence payers, i.e. almost everyone)
9   Taxpayers' aid to private energy firm
10   Couples disagree on purse strings/relationship
10   Poetry prize (hard to categorize – but relevant to poetry readers)
12   Magic mushroom ban
12   Lottery jackpot

HUMAN INTEREST – ORDINARY PEOPLE

8   Parents commit suicide after son's suicide
14   Poker win
16   Asylum seeker freed (nib)

QUIRKS

7   Nude art
12   Fast food/pigeons
12   Exotic plants struggle in Surrey
14   Poaching leads to tuskless elephants

THE INDEPENDENT

CONFLICT

POLITICS

CELEBS

HUMAN INTEREST – RELEVANCE TO THE READER

HUMAN INTEREST – ORDINARY PEOPLE

QUIRKS

RESEARCH, SCIENCE, DISCOVERY

DAILY TELEGRAPH

CONFLICT

1	London bombs link with Iraq invasion
4	London bombs investigation
4	London bomber used gyms to enlist disaffected youths
4	London bombs link with Iraq continued
4	London bombs victims
4	Biochemist admits having keys to suspected bomb factory
5	Turkey bombs vigil for victims
5	Turkey bombs tourists not put off
5	Iraq bombs tactics
6	Iraq Saddam charges plus analysis
6	Iraq bombs soldiers named
d10	Teen murder charge
10	Shot man had gun licence revoked
10	Speedboat collision
13	Sharon's tanks on Gaza edge
14	Spain's forest fire
14	Hurricane Emily
14	Thai clampdown on rebels

POLITICS

1	Edward Heath dies
2/3	Heath (picture/tribute spread)
6	Iraq/Iran relationship
6	Iraq book censored by Downing Street
8	Tory moderates attack Davis's tax cuts
8	Government incentives for teenagers
10	European wine = green glass UK headache
12	Army recruitment shortage
13	Chirac free air trip row
14	Aceh peace deal

CELEBS

7	*Charlie and the Chocolate Factory* premiere
8	Camilla's coat of arms
11	Harry Potter launch

HUMAN INTEREST – RELEVANCE TO THE READER

9	Maternity ward risks
9	US firm sued after faulty cataract lenses ruin eyesight
9	Research shows children are no strain on future marriages
10	Biggest shoplifters are men
10	Sheep dip wipes out insect river life
11	Drivers flunk recognition tests
14	Redefining motherhood – women picking up guitars

HUMAN INTEREST – ORDINARY PEOPLE

QUIRKS

THE TIMES

CONFLICT

POLITICS

20   Government campaign to dilute impact of student fees
31   Indonesia/Aceh conflict near resolution
30   Bush Adviser CIA identity leak

CELEBS
1   Tiger Woods' open win
1   Harry Potter figures
4   Jude Law affair
10   Harry Potter reading
22   Globe puts on Shakespeare in original entirety
22   Zadie Smith husband nominated for poet prize
24   Camilla's birthday arms

HUMAN INTEREST – RELEVANCE TO THE READER
4   Vets check for bird disease
5   London Zoo to get rid of cages
12   Drivers want speed cameras to carry a speed limit sign
12   Libraries risk becoming relics
13   Neighbour wars = 1/10 move
18   Catholic families want church to combat material pressures
21   Anti-fat drug – doctors who use it refused insurance
21   Junior doctors exams/working hours
24   Heatwave forecast
24   House prices fall

HUMAN INTEREST – ORDINARY PEOPLE
4   Parents commit suicide after son's suicide
29   Poker win
29   Asylum seeker gets visa
21   Bubonic plague tests on scientists for anti-terrorism (nib)

QUIRKS
4   Fast food = giant pigeons
12   Nude art
21   Laughing gas in chocolate
29   HK to send bodies to China for lack of funeral space
31   Elephants' evolution – lose tusks to beat poachers
31   Evolution sped up by human meddling (Sidebar)

SCIENCE, RESEARCH, DISCOVERY
23   Rerouting of NASA probe

DAILY EXPRESS

CONFLICT
1   London bombs investigation
4/5   Soldiers killed in Iraq (spread)
4   Suicide bombers in Iraq
6/7   London bombs (spread with four related stories)

8/9	Turkey bombs, British victims (spread plus sidebar)
19	Hurricane Emily
19	Woodland fire deaths in Spain (nib)
19	Saddam charges (nib)

POLITICS

1	Ted Heath dies (picture cross reference)
2	Heath (full story)
24/25	Heath (obituary/tribute spread)

CELEBS

1	Jude Law affair teaser
12	Harry Potter launch and review (sidebar)
13	*Charlie and the Chocolate Factory* premiere
16/17	Jude Law affair (spread)

HUMAN INTEREST – RELEVANCE TO THE READER

2	Clinic can give contraception to children of 12
2	Risks in maternity wards, according to watchdog
2	Investigation into deaths in police chases
15	Pensioners run up credit card debts
21	Drivers clueless about road signs

HUMAN INTEREST ORDINARY PEOPLE

| 22 | Man gets compost bin after Express campaign |

QUIRKS

| 3 | Nude art – 1,500 people strip naked in Newcastle |
| 23 | ATM fraudsters leave photos of themselves |

DAILY MAIL

CONFLICT

1	London bombs Iraq link (splash)
2	London bombs Iraq link (splash contd)
5	Girl, 14, on stabbing charge (nib)
8/9	London bombs investigation (spread)
8/9	Did London bombers intend to die? (spread)
8	Iraq suicide bombs
9	Iraq bombs deaths of British soldiers
10	Bomb-proof battle bus for terror police
10/11	Background/feature on Leeds Muslims
14	Turkey bomb – British victim

POLITICS

2	Blair censors envoy's book
5	Alan Duncan drops bid for Tory leadership
6	Tributes to Ted Heath

10	Failure to deport asylum-seekers (also *conflict*)
18/19	Background/feature/obituary Heath
21	Government plan for bribes to yobs to stay out of trouble
25	Ministers on the spot over enforced collapse of Railtrack

CELEBS

1	Jude Law/Sienna (picture cross ref)
3	Jude Law affair
3	Hugh Grant/Jemima Khan/Liz Hurley triangle
7	Victoria Beckham has a night out
7	Kylie Minogue flies to Paris for cancer treatment

HUMAN INTEREST – RELEVANCE TO THE READER

4	Risks on maternity wards
5	Investigation into deaths in police car crashes
20	Rip off rates for phones for hospital patients
22/23	Climate confusion (picture spread)
25	Possible danger in some skin creams

HUMAN INTEREST – ORDINARY PEOPLE

30	Couple's suicide after son's suicide
29	Operation called off
31	Sick baby has outing

QUIRKS

15	Rail chaos caused by stray cow (nib)
15	Plague of locusts in France (nib)
21	Nude art
31	Fast food waste creates overweight super pigeons

RESEARCH, SCIENCE, DISCOVERY

| 20 | Sales campaign for blackcurrants |
| 29 | Scampi suffer from stress |

DAILY MIRROR

CONFLICT

1	London bomber bought perfume to make bombs
2	Iraq suicide bombs
M2	British troops to come home from Iraq in six months
2	Saddam trial nears
4/5	London bombers (spread)
4	MI5 error over bomber
4	Mum of bomb victim
4	Fund for bomb victims
6	Terrorism training clamp down in Pakistan
6	Profiles of bomb victims
7	London bombs investigation

POLITICS

CELEBS

HUMAN INTEREST – RELEVANCE TO THE READER

HUMAN INTEREST – ORDINARY PEOPLE

QUIRKS

DAILY STAR

QUIRKS
12   Nude art
15   Laughing gas in chocolate

THE SUN

CONFLICT
1   London bombs shop link (write-off)
6   London bombs shop link (full story)
6   London bombs chemist 'grandson' of Christian priest
8/9   London bomber father
9   London bombs death toll
10   Iraq bombs soldier tribute
10   Iraq troops out in a year
11   Turkey bombs British victim
27   Three die in crash
27   Body found in boot
28   Boat crash

POLITICS
2   Edward Heath dies (report and analysis)
6   Anti-terror law
19   Government 'bribes' to yobs

CELEBS
1   Jude Law affair (write-off)
4/5   Jude Law affair (full story)
7   Amir Khan promotes unity
14/15   Harry Potter launch
17   Coleen parking row
24   Chef repeatedly fired after Gordon Ramsay programme
27   BBC role for Calil
27   Corrie stars' car trouble

HUMAN INTEREST - RELEVANCE TO THE READER
19   Maternity ward risks
28   Staff would like financial incentive to travel by scooter/motorbike

HUMAN INTEREST - ORDINARY PEOPLE
17   Parents commit suicide after son's suicide
18   Nursery lost child
25   Britons like sex on holiday

RESEARCH, SCIENCE, DISCOVERY
18   Men prefer offices to be cooler (nib)

QUIRKS

3	Nude art
19	Dishwasher thief on camera
27	Meteor showers mistaken for distress flares (nib)

TUESDAY JULY 19

THE GUARDIAN

CONFLICT

1	Foreign scientists banned amid terror fears
1	London bombs Pakistan militants linked
2	UK court convicts Afghan warlord
2	Foreign scientists barred (continued)
3	Milwall v Iran possibly called off amid racism fears
4	Germany blocks extradition of terror suspect
5	London bombings – poll says 2/3 believe Iraq linked
5	London bombs tributes
5	Ex-IRA man calls for better security on buses
5	Blair help plea to Muslim leaders
6	River death boy named (nib)
6	England fans – trial unfair (Portugal)
6	Teacher in child porn case
6	Fishermen rescued from sinking boat
7	Man who stole underwear/sex aids faces jail
7	Girl, 12, hangs boy, 5
7	Woman sentenced for infecting boyfriend with HIV
7	Australia recruits British squaddies
8	Baby may have been buried alive
12	Rape claim policeman re-arrested
12	Man jailed for parrot beheading
13	Israeli protests defy police ban
14	Milosevic aides jailed for murder of former Serb president
14	Amnesty International call for Spanish civil war justice
14	Atlanta bomber jailed for abortion clinic blast
15	Iraq police numbers to double

POLITICS

4	Cross-party backing on Clarke terror laws
4	Plea bargaining urged to gain terror info
8	Widdecombe and Galloway unite to stop deportation
9	Ministers deny teen smartcards are covert id
9	Home Office will miss aslyum targets
11	Tory MPs vote on rules for leader
11	Ex spin doctor's book faces ban
11	Kennedy by-election success

POLITICS

CELEBS

HUMAN INTEREST – RELEVANCE TO THE READER

HUMAN INTEREST – ORDINARY PEOPLE

QUIRKS

DAILY TELEGRAPH

CONFLICT

10   Afghan warlord convicted
10   Woman jailed for infecting boyfriend with HIV
11   Baby buried alive in concrete
11   Girl, 12, tries to hang boy, 5
13   Sharon foils mass protest
13   Getty curator turned blind eye to archaeology theft
14   Ex Serbian president's assassin jailed
14   Hurricane Emily
14   Guantanamo trials go-ahead
14   Atlanta Olympics bomber jailed

POLITICS
1   Countryside under threat in Prescott homes plan
2   Countryside under threat (continued)
2   Brown delays spending details in power struggles
8   Edward Heath tributes
8   Tories oppose Howard vote plans
13   Bush retreats in CIA leak affair
15   Mugabe plea for South African aid

CELEBS
5   Polanski trial
7   Euan Blair graduates
9   Jude Law affair

HUMAN INTEREST - RELEVANCE TO THE READER
2   Fifth of ready-made salads too salty
2   Asylum rejects costs to taxpayers
3   French women lead as mothers, workers, lovers
6   48-hour promise on GPs not met
7   2/3 want to spend money not leave inheritance
9   BBC chief promises to prevent bad language

HUMAN INTEREST - ORDINARY PEOPLE
7   Policemen sacked for racist text joke
11   Farmers pay price for over-order of foreign barbecue steaks
15   Threat to Pacific islands as inhabitants move on

QUIRKS
10   Device to measure angle of caber toss
14   Church moves to 16,000 seater stadium to accommodate congregation
15   Escaped panda

THE TIMES

CONFLICT
2   Man jailed for beheading parrot in front of family
4   Gunman jailed (nib)

4	Boy, 7, drowns (nib)
7	Woman jailed for infecting boyfriend with HIV
8	London bombers met plotter in Pakistan
8/9	Blair appeals for Muslim backing on terror laws
9	MI5 sent out for covert neighbourhood watch
13	Girl 12, tried to hang boy, 5
19	Baby buried in concrete
22	Afghan warlord convicted
22	Warlord used 'human dog' to terrorise
26	German court frees terror suspect
27	Secret police convicted of former Serb president's murder (nib)
27	Atlanta bomber jailed for life (nib)
27	Lebanese anti-Syrian leader to be freed (nib)
28	Israeli protestors defy ban
28	Hurricane Emily
28	Northern Ireland peace plans copied by Basque terror group
28	Arsonists firebomb teapot headquarters of Malaysian cult
30	Iraq ayatollah condemns suicide bombers
30	World Bank giant loan to fund Iraq basic services

POLITICS

1	Asylum chaos
2	Brown delays spending review
2	Brown review analysis
2	Charles Kennedy's change in tax plans (nib)
4	Lords reform plans
4	Tory revolt on leadership vote plus analysis
7	Government says media harms army recruitment (nib)
11	Plan to reward well-behaved teens
20	Bar diversity threatened by Lord Chancellor
23	Japan accused of buying votes for whale hunting
27	German social democrat scandal – Volkswagen paid for sex parties
27	First presidential poll to be held in Egypt (nib)
29	Poll shows most don't want Turkey in EU
31	Bush's fancy dinner for Indian prime minister
31	Mugabe asks South Africa for £1bn

CELEBS

3	Polanski trial
4	Ali G star offends US family
20	Moore sculpture up for auction
22	British mission to Mars professor has MS
22	Lennon's replica youth items in museum (nib)

HUMAN INTEREST – RELEVANT TO THE READER

2	Farmland tax plan
2	New BBC director of sport (nib)
4	One fifth of ready made salads too salty (nib)
4	Average British woman spends £31,000 on shoes in lifetime (nib)
5	Train company: too hot for air conditioning

23	Man jailed for decapitating parrot
26	Terror gang still on loose
26	Israeli police block demo
26	11 firemen dead from forest fire
27	Firms fleeced by conmen

POLITICS

2	Blair leads Heath tributes
2	Plan to reward teens for good behaviour
4	283,500 failed asylum seekers in Britain

CELEBS

5	Polanski court case
5	Jude Law affair
21	Zeta Jones's Monroe disguise
21	Jonathan Ross's new rural retreat
26	Prince Albert's new lovechild
27	Katie Derham's baby

HUMAN INTEREST – RELEVANCE TO THE READER

2	GP access struggle
10	Women's shoe spending
15	Road deaths rise in speed camera areas
20	Singing helps safer driving
22	Wine drinkers fitter, happier, cleverer

HUMAN INTEREST – ORDINARY PEOPLE

10	Mum with 14 kids
19	Police sacked over racist texts
23	Family suicide

QUIRKS

3	Swan-upping
20	Seven hour delay because train hit cow
23	Woman passes driving test after 33 years

DAILY MAIL

CONFLICT

8	London bombers – Pakistan terror school
8	London bombs Blair denies Iraq link
8	Camera system in Pakistan airport matched bombers
9	Cleric 'suicide sympathiser' visit
19	Iraq's neighbourhood militias
20	Girl, 12, attempted to hang boy, 5
25	Hurricane Emily
10	Afghan warlord; £30,000/year of taxpayers' money to keep him in jail
32	Baby buried alive in concrete

POLITICS

2	Countryside fears Prescott house plans
6	128,500 asylum rejects vanish from files
6	Clarke postpones deportation of Zimbabweans
9	Clarke's new terror laws
35	MPs to debate abortion limit cut

CELEBS

2	Chinese Rover bid (unclassifiable, but put here because it is a famous firm)
4/5	Polanski in court
7	Madonna feeds chickens (photos)
11	Prince Wills/girlfriend Kate in Kenya
12/13	Jude Law affair
21	Rod Stewart/Penny Lancaster go sailing
27	Harry Potter sales

HUMAN INTEREST – RELEVANCE TO THE READER

1	GP access struggle
4	GP story continued
19	Rich families get tax credits
19	Delay on Alzheimer drug ruling
21	Post office removes pay-for-cash machines
26	Pensioners opt for good life instead of leaving inheritance
26	Couples don't know each other, study says
28	Women's shoe spending
31	Speed camera road deaths
33	Ready made salads too salty
33	Wine buffs healthier, cleverer
33b	Fish oils important for children

HUMAN INTEREST – ORDINARY PEOPLE

3	Mum has 14 children
25	Cancer for 23-year-old sunbed user
25	18-year-old sets up airline
27	Teen lottery winner through with men, but having boob job
31	Family suicide
32	Woman who infected lover with HIV jailed
35	Police race sackings: double standards

QUIRKS

15	Fly swatting research
40/41	Nude art
25	Peacocks plague village

THE MIRROR

CONFLICT

| 1 | Hanging girl: other victim's story (write-off) |
| 2 | Hatfield firm guilty |

POLITICS

CELEBS

HUMAN INTEREST – RELEVANCE TO THE READER

HUMAN INTEREST – ORDINARY PEOPLE

QUIRKS

3	Sit ups for porn watchers in India (nib)
7	Snail race world champion (nib)
8	Scrap dealer pays £60k for 'scr4p' plate (nib)
31	Mystery nude weekly run through Manchester high street
31	Jellyfish invasion for Costa tourists

DAILY STAR

CONFLICT

7	London bombs investigation – suspects vanish
7	Turkey bombs tribute
7	Fury at cleric's speech
12	Hurricane Emily
13	Woman jailed for infecting man with HIV
18	Baby buried alive in concrete block
20	Girl,12, nearly kills boy, 5, in hanging
21	Lotto lout in jail

POLITICS

2	Failed asylum seekers still in UK
2	Teen bribes government row

CELEBS

1	Death threat to Big Brother's Craig (write-off)
3	Jude Law affair
3	Harry Potter sales
3	Jonathan Ross rural retreat
3	Darker new series of *Desperate Housewives*
3	James Hewitt in poker show
4	Ali G star offends US family
4/5	Lee Sharpe/Abi Titmuss
8/9	Craig death threat
8/9	*Big Brother* four stories
14	Beckham in LA
15	BBC chief likes new *Dr Who*
15	Justin Timberlake charity basketball
15	Ninja Turtles new film
23	Model pics from film shooting

HUMAN INTEREST – RELEVANCE TO THE READER

13	Women bare more flesh
13	Hatfeld rail firm admits mistakes
13	Job satisfaction slump (nib)
14	Cancer hell for sunbed lover nurse
23	More crash deaths in speed camera areas
20	Women spend average £31,000 on shoes in a lifetime (nib)

HUMAN INTEREST – ORDINARY PEOPLE

6	18-year-old launches airline
15	Police sacked for racist text joke

THE SUN

CONFLICT

1	Muslim cleric UK visit (write-off)
2	Spain's forest fire
4	Baby buried alive in block
6	Girl, 12, hangs boy of 5
6	£3m taxpayers' bill to cage warlord
7	RAF lieutenant jailed for sexual abuse on girl
8/9	London bombers bonded on outdoor pursuits
8	London bombs death toll
9	London bombs chemist could be freed by Egypt
10	Turkey bomb victim
10/11	Muslim cleric visit to Britain
11	London bombs Iraq link denied
12	BBC attacked for showing warlord's Iraq rant
16	Hurricane Emily
15	Yob Lotto winner faces jail
18	Woman jailed for intentionally infecting man with HIV
19	Eurofighter jet narrow escape
24	Man jailed for biting head off parrot
27	Yugoslav ex-soldiers accused of shooting Britons
29	Woman convicted of helping paedophile husband
29	Hatfield rail firm admits to blunders

POLITICS

2	300,000 rejected asylum seekers still in UK
2	UK support for EU the lowest

CELEBS

1	Jude Law affair (write-off)
2	Chinese Rover bid
3	Jessie Wallace leaving *Eastenders*
3	Harry Potter sales
3	Jonathan Ross new home
4	Mars mission professor has MS
4/5	Jude Law affair
5	Jude Law affair
7	Penny Lancaster pregant (pics)
7	Euan Blair graduation
18	Beckham chats to woman
19	Ninja turtles film (nib)
19	Kylie has ovaries frozen
19	Cat Deeley and Patrick Kielty seen together
25	Wills's Kenyan love nest with Kate

27   Ginola found with weapon gift at airport
29   Yorkshire Ripper ill due to biscuit binge (celeb obviously not the right word, but he is
        undoubtedly here because he is famous)
29   Jolie's new baby

HUMAN INTEREST – RELEVANCE TO THE READER
2   340,000 parents waiting to be dealt with by CSA
7   Women bare 50 per cent more flesh than a decade ago (nib)
15   Road deaths rise in areas with more speed cameras
18   Alzheimer drugs delayed
22   Women spend £31,680 on shoes in lifetime
24   10 health trusts axe free IVF treatment
24   Wine drinkers healthier and cleverer
25   Ready made salads – too much salt
25   Smokers more likely to lose teeth (nib)
27   Job satisfaction slumps 10 per cent in past three years
28   Cancer patients – expensive parking/trips to hospitals
30   Survey reveals singing = safer driving (nib)

HUMAN INTEREST – ORDINARY PEOPLE
4   Woman has 14 kids
14   18-year-old launches airline
27   Family suicide
29   OAP a pub regular for 72 years
30   Police sacked for racist texts
22   Fish kills boy in Malaysia (nib)

QUIRKS
15   ITN gives porn link on lunchtime news
15   Stag party gatecrashes *Songs of Praise* recording (nib)
16   Sit ups for Indian porn watchers (nib)
16   Snail racing win (nib)
16/17   Nude art
18   Dad runs around UK with orange on head to promote exercise for young
19   Drinking prankster sets fire to pal's bum
28   Train standstill after it hits a cow

INDEX